Tales from the Tiger Rag

compiled and edited by

Michael Jones

Pen Press

First published in Great Britain by Pen Press

All paper used in the printing of this book has been made from wood grown in managed, sustainable forests.

ISBN13: 978-1-78003-050-0

Printed and bound in the UK
Pen Press is an imprint of Indepenpress Publishing Limited
25 Eastern Place
Brighton
BN2 1GJ

A catalogue record of this book is available from the British Library

Cover design by Jacqueline Abromeit

Contents

Introduction 1

The Origins of the Tiger Club 3

The Rollason Turbulent 8

Tiger Tag or Formation Aerobatics 14

The very last Touring Air Show 20

Stampes in Grande Bretagne - Early Days 25

Accidents and Incidents 30

The Arrival of the Cosmic Wind 34

An Easter Monday 39

A Turbulent Story 43

A Turbulent Sea Story 47

Unusual Types 51

The Caithness Saga 55

A Tiger's Tale or a Check Pilot's Nightmare. 59

Golf Courses 64

Messing about in Boats 68

The Toothpick 71

Displays Abroad 76

Reno 'The Empire Strikes Back' 80

Confessions 84

Aviation or Flying? 90

Introduction

The Tiger Club newsletter adopted its title of 'Tiger Rag' in January 1961 when Lewis (Benjy) Benjamin volunteered both to produce and edit it. In the very early years the Club secretary and C.F.I C. Nepean Bishop (Bish) produced what were known as 'Bulletins' which although containing essential information about the new Club were rather short and a little infrequent. Benjy approached his task with energy and enthusiasm and insisted not only on a monthly publication but also on six closely typed foolscap pages. Under Benjy's editorship the Rag was always written on a typewriter and duplicated from stencils by devoted people either in Putney where Benjy lived or later in Reigate close to Redhill aerodrome. It was only in 1981 when Benjy finally retired as editor that the Rag conceded to photographs and modern technology.

In effect Benjy turned a newsletter into a magazine. It always consisted of contributions from Club members together with Benjy's regular and very personal editorial which usually contained appropriate comments about the flying weather at Redhill. Letters, quotes, jokes, comments and long articles about touring flights and expeditions flowed in from members and the Rag was only very rarely short of copy. It provided a special link with members based overseas and reminded them not only of home but their chosen sporting activity. For a time an aerobatics newsletter was added to the publication giving results and details of aerobatic competitions organised by the Club.

The contribution from Benjy to this collection at his suggestion has been slightly revised but all the other articles in this book were originally printed in the Tiger Rag. Some but by no means all have been reproduced in three volumes of the Club's history already in print. In the attempt to be both informative and enjoyable the selection has been particularly difficult. Also after much reflection I have decided not to produce accompanying photographs and illustrations. They did not contribute to the success of the original Rags and plenty of prints have been already featured in the volumes mentioned above.

In this book the 'Tales' have not been listed in any special order but their authors have been noted. My warmest thanks and acknowledgements are due to Club members both past and present for their contributions.

Finally I am very grateful to Inge Work Clausen for allowing me to use her computer and her expertise to produce the manuscript.

Michael Jones – President The Tiger Club.

The Origins of the Tiger Club

In 2006 the Tiger Club celebrated its 50th anniversary. To commemorate the event a garden party was held at Headcorn and a lunch at the RAF Club in London. Many people asked: How did it all begin? Michael Jones supplies some of the answers.

The answer may be history, legend or even simple nostalgia. The nuances are not important. Some people said that the idea was first discussed in 1955. Chris Wren who designed the Club's logo thought that the Club was founded 'late in 1956'; he may have been referring to the Club's first so called annual general meeting which took place at the Royal Aero Club on 23rd November that year. Lewis (Benjy) Benjamin who wrote the first two volumes of the Club's history says that it was on 24th January 1956 at an end of season air racing dinner held at the Royal Aero Club and this seems to be the generally accepted date. A document exists which unfortunately is neither signed nor dated but which was almost certainly written by Norman Jones. It states as follows:

SUGGESTED FORMATION OF THE TIGER CLUB

Aims of the Club are:

1.) To provide the means of meeting for those who take

an active part in Tiger Moth racing and aerobatics.

2.) To encourage and regulate Tiger Moth racing and aerobatics.

3.) To organise an annual dinner and any other function which may be thought useful.

4.) To present annually a tiger skin flying helmet to the most successful Tiger Moth racer of the year who will bear the title of 'Tiger Tim'.

The document then went on to list the six founder members which included Chris Wren and Norman Jones and to state that additional members were only to be admitted if proposed and seconded by founder members. Finally it laid down that the annual subscription would be 10/- 'for the time being'.

Can one detect a note of exasperation in the suggestions made in this document which was obviously written after a good party? Were people dissatisfied with the way air racing and aerobatics were being organised at an official level? Could the annual dinner have been better? Were Tiger Moths being unfairly handicapped in the national air races? These questions are of course pure speculation and it is more than probable that the whole project was originally undertaken in a very light hearted spirit.

C. Nepean Bishop (Bish) was one of the first members to be admitted to the happy band. Bish had met up with Norman Jones at the Surrey Flying Club which was based at Croydon Airport and he was immediately appointed Hon. Secretary and C.F.I. to the embryonic Club. He was soon in touch with the Air Registration Board (ARB) and in May 1956 he wrote seeking permission to carry out a falling leaf manoeuvre in a Tiger Moth entered in a forthcoming aerobatic competition. He was reminded by the ARB that permission was not required and that all aerobatics might legally be undertaken in a Tiger Moth with a C of A in the aerobatic category but that 'outside loops, bunts, and flick manoeuvres should not be carried out on any civil aircraft'.

With a little prompting from Norman Jones, Bish was not the sort of person to let the grass grow under his feet. At the end of 1956 he entered into a long correspondence with officials of the Royal Aero Club over his intention to organise 'silver jubilee meetings' for Tiger Moths early in 1957. The first was for closed circuit racing at Sandown on Easter Monday and the second an aerobatic competition for pilots of 'limited experience' at Sywell in May. However he was firmly reminded by the Royal Aero Club that he would need an 'Organising Permit' for both these events issued by the Royal Aero Club in accordance with the Sporting Code of the Federation Aeronautique Internationale (FAI). It was obvious that one of the original suggested aims that of 'regulating Tiger Moth racing and aerobatics' might be difficult to achieve in practice and in fact this paragraph was removed from the aims of the Club shortly afterwards. Both these events at Sandown and Sywell were a great success and at the end of 1957 the Club could boast a membership of 47.

Curiously enough although another Tiger Moth closed circuit race meeting was organised in 1958, the idea seemed to fade although there was plenty of enthusiasm for the National Handicap Races organised by the Royal aero Club. This was ironic because it was Tiger Moth racing pilots who had started the Club in the first place. But for aerobatics it was a different story; apparently 'organising permits' were no longer required and the arrival of the Super Tiger complete with inverted fuel and oil system made all the difference. The fact that this aircraft was capable of carrying out all those manoeuvres which the ARB said should not be carried out excited no comment, particularly as Club members entered the machine for the international Lockheed Trophy and it was later used by the French national champion. 1958 incidentally saw the inauguration of the De Havilland and Esso Tiger trophy competitions with some very welcome sponsorship. As a result of all this and the introduction of other activities such as display flying, touring, glider towing and parachute dropping by the end of 1958 membership had increased to 101.

As for the original suggested aims the tiger skin flying helmet survived for a couple of years and then was quietly dropped. Probably the idea was considered too trivial for what had by then become a more serious organisation. The first aim was expanded to include displays and other forms of competition and the words 'light aeroplane' replaced the words 'Tiger Moth'. The reason for this was only too obvious. A French Druine Turbulent had made a demonstration tour of British flying clubs in 1956 and had excited the interest of Norman Jones. Also the appearance of the Stampe at the Lockheed Trophy had impressed many aerobatic enthusiasts. In I957 two new paragraphs were added to the aims of the Club: (1) 'To provide its members with good sporting flying at the lowest possible cost' and (2) 'To work for improvement in standards of light aeroplane flying, aerobatics and private flying generally'. For some reason or other the aim of organising an annual dinner was dropped later but this has not stopped the Club from holding an annual dinner every year without fail ever since! Finally from the very beginning a Committee and a constitution of sorts was established and most important of all a charter which every new member signed and was printed in the very first Club membership book: 'A member of the Club undertakes: (1) Always to go out of their way to assist others in aeronautical matters, (2) Always to fly with courtesy and special attention to the safety and comfort of others and (3) Never to use an aeroplane for a disreputable or unworthy purpose'.

It may well be asked how the Club managed to survive and expand in those very early years without a proper base to carry out essential checks and familiarisation since the permanent base at Redhill aerodrome was not established until late in 1959. True some flying was done from Croydon airport where Norman Jones' company Rollasons had their premises, but the airport was under sentence of closure and being controlled did not suit most people. The answer lay in the establishment of various branches up and down southern England. These existed at Fairoaks, Sywell, Little Snoring and even Ramsgate. The branch at Fairoaks was particularly important. A small blister hangar was leased which could house three or four Tiger Moths and a lot of flying was done from there. Sometimes these branches caused administrative headaches to the Chairman and the Committee but the Club relied heavily on its Charter.

The Rollason Turbulent

The Rollason Turbulent celebrated its 50th anniversary in 2008. The little ultra-light single seater has played such a large part in the history of the Tiger Club that its story is well worth recalling by Michael Jones.

The prototype Rollason Turbulent G-APBZ was flown on its maiden flight by Norman Jones from Croydon Airport on New Year's Day 1958. Of course G-APBZ was in fact an example of a Druine Turbulent which first flew in France in 1953. The machine in question F-PGYQ won the prize at the RSA rally that year for the best amateur constructed aircraft in France. Roger Druine had already built and flown his first aircraft while still a teenager and his Turbulent design won immediate acclaim amongst the home building fraternity in France so much so in fact that another amateur built version nicknamed Napoleon was loaned for a demonstration tour of British flying clubs in 1956. The Druine Turbulent was quickly and enthusiastically adopted by the PFA for amateur builders in Britain and Norman Jones wasted no time in obtaining Roger Druine's agreement for Rollasons to produce the Turbulent under licence. Tragically 1958 also saw the early death of Roger Druine from leukaemia but happily close contact was maintained with his charming widow Marcelle who lived in Paris.

Thus the Rollason Turbulent project which included the Ardem engine was born. A first batch of ten machines was laid down, most of which eventually found their way to the Tiger Club's hangar at Redhill following the Club's move there in 1959 when Croydon was finally closed. These ten Turbulents had registrations beginning with the letters AP and ending in Z and one other was sold a retired RAF Air Commodore Chris Paul who insisted on his own personal registration ending with the letters CP.

There was a further connection with the RAF because at this time the Tiger Club was fortunate that two active serving Squadron Leaders applied to join – John Severne and Clive Francis. Both were exceptional pilots and both fell in love with the Rollason Turbulent. The immediate results were that in 1959 John Severne who had been appointed equerry to the Duke of Edinburgh persuaded HRH to have flight in G-APNZ at White Waltham and in 1960 G-APNZ entered by Prince Philip and flown by John Severne won the King's Cup with G-APZZ flown by Clive Francis coming second. Soon Clive Francis became, so to speak, the founding father of the Club's Turbulent formation team and was responsible for organising the nine ship formation displays which took place on the public days at the 1961 Farnborough Air Show. It was rumoured that Clive had once flown a Club Turbulent through an RAF hangar so, it was said, to improve the morale of his squadron, an exploit, it was also said, did not advance his career in the RAF! Clive later became the official RAF schools recruiting officer and it was agreed that he could use a Club Turbulent equipped with stick-on RAF roundels from time to time for his liaison visits. Then there was another link with the RAF because Turbulent G-APIZ was loaned to the RAF College Flying Club at Cranwell where it was well utilised by the cadets.

However alongside these considerable publicity and promotional triumphs there were set backs. In 1957 a disturbing report was received at Croydon that a French built Turbulent had lost a wing in flight killing a top level aerobatic pilot, Francois d'Huc Dressler. It was alleged that he had been doing aerobatics. The Druine Turbulent had never been designed to be aerobatic and its extremely light finger and thumb stick forces which made it such a delight to fly normally would lead it to be easily overstressed if aerobatics were performed. Also when the first Turbulent arrived at the Tiger Club it was ignored by some of the senior members; they said that it was not a real aeroplane; with only a 30 HP converted car engine it was under powered; it was only a toy and anyway their personal insurance policies would not allow them to fly a single seat aeroplane issued only with a Permit to Fly. They preferred the good old Tiger Moth issued with a C of A! Then again at two of the first air shows at which the Rollason Turbulent was demonstrated, Sandown and Barton, G-APBZ and G-APMZ had been badly damaged in accidents almost certainly caused by over-confidence. Both aircraft were rebuilt using the same registrations; it was always Norman's policy to rebuild aircraft even if effectively destroyed in accidents if the pilot survived to tell the tale! Finally worst of all, G-APKZ, that had been sold to the Biggin Hill Flying Club as a new aircraft late in 1960 lost a wing while performing aerobatics in the vicinity of Biggin Hill, inevitably killing the pilot who had already been warned against doing aerobatics in a Turbulent. But Norman Jones was undismayed by these disasters and Rollasons laid down another batch of ten Turbulents whose registrations started with the letters AR and again ended with a Z. His only reaction was to order that the following notice was to be fitted to the panels of all aircraft of the Tiger Club: 'ALL AIRCRAFT BITE FOOLS'!

Although the Turbulent was a very welcome source of cheap flying for Tiger Club members and popular for formation sorties and displays as well as touring, the numbers of aircraft being turned out by Rollasons in the early sixties began to exceed the Club's requirements and sales of new machines were few and far between. Consequently new initiatives were taken to promote the Turbulent to the wider sporting aviation public. The catalogue price of a 'standard' Turbulent with 1192 cc engine in 1960 was £950 but Rollasons also offered a 'de luxe' version with 1500 cc engine, wheel spats, sliding cockpit canopy, brakes and hand starter for £1250. The idea was to improve the appearance and potential of the aircraft for touring. Unfortunately there were only few takers for the 'de luxe' version although one aircraft was shipped to the USA and G-APBZ having been rebuilt and modified after another mishap was sold in this form to the Air Touring Club at Biggin Hill.

However further initiatives followed usually with the help of Tiger Club enthusiasts: a 'Tallboy' Turbulent for members with unreasonably long legs, a Turbulent on skis, a great success providing there was enough snow, a Turbulent on floats, it worked but only just, a glider towing Turbulent just to prove the point, a Turbulent fitted with an extra fuel tank and radio for a flight to Australia, it never got very far. Various altitude records, the Dawn to Dusk competition invented originally specifically for Turbulents and plenty of other ideas. Finally in an attempt to persuade ordinary flying clubs and schools to buy the Turbulent, Rollasons decided to launch the aircraft with a full C of A. The project was very expensive and negotiations with the ARB seemed endless and when eventually G-ARLZ appeared with a modified spar, trim tab and heavier stick forces, ordinary flying clubs were still not persuaded. Worse when Tiger Club aficionados flew G-ARLZ they did not like it; it was heavier and had lost some of the Turbulent magic; they preferred the original Druine version. But one major benefit emerged from this whole exercise for Rollasons; Frank Hounslow after much toil and patience obtained the necessary type certificate for the Ardem engine and it was eventually sold in quantity to the RAF via Slingsby for the Venture powered glider used by ATC squadrons.

If calculations are correct, Rollason's final tally of Turbulents was 30. Of these 27 were the original D31 type and only 3 the D31A C of A version. And of these 30 at least 18 have been operated at one time or another by the Tiger Club. These figures do not of course include quite a few rebuilds of machines retaining their original registration. The last airframe to be built under the Rollason banner was G-BIVZ manufactured down at Rye under the personal supervision of Norman Jones who was then well into his retirement.

This then is a very brief account of the Rollason Turbulent story. Now that the type is more than fifty years old and continues to be operated with great success by the Tiger Club its claim to the status of a classic ultra light aeroplane is fully justified. It is also a tribute to its designer Roger Druine and to Rollasons and Norman Jones who sponsored its series production. Also the Turbulent has fulfilled and continues to fulfil one of the Tiger Club's original aims which was 'to provide its members with good sporting flying at the lowest possible cost'. True there have been mishaps probably too many that could and should have been avoided and the type which as Roger Druine put it was a 'design for youth' has a tendency to breed overconfidence. On the other hand the Turbulent is a delightful and attractive aircraft which encourages airmanship, enterprise and adventure and will continue to do so for many years to come.

Tiger Tag or Formation Aerobatics

Neil Williams in his note to this contribution said it was 'as seen on the day from the No 3 position'. The Tigers were the Super Tigers – NZZ, OAA, and NMZ.

So far, so good; just another formation take-off. Looking to my right I can see Peter's head moving from side to side as he positions us for the start of the display. Beyond him a black and silver Tiger is glued to his wing tip; from there James looks like a bearded Viking – pity he hasn't got horns on his helmet! The waiting is the worst as we gain height. And it's so easy to hold position too, when Peter turns with only 20° of bank! Oh well, if he kept it down to that it wouldn't be an aerobatic formation! Hullo, this is it, here we go; Peter looks at each of us in turn and we nod confidently, (liar, in my case; I never felt less confident about anything!) Again Peter signals making a circular motion with his hand (we know he is going to start with a loop but with no R/T we've decided to retain all hand signals).

I ease the trimmer fully forward – I find it helps to hold a steady pull force, and as Peter nods his head we ease forward into the dive. I have full power and I'm only just holding him – and he's supposed to be flying the slowest aircraft! Surely we might be approaching 120 knots if the roar of the slipstream is anything to go by. There is an almost overwhelming temptation to glance at my ASI, but sure as fate if I do that I'll be on my own! My aircraft has eased up a couple of feet and I can see James on the other side of Peter's fin and rudder. He appears to be completely at ease and is as steady as a rock. Very gently I press forward on the stick and start easing down into position, and of course this is the moment when Peter nods again and two aircraft leap forwards away from me! I pull hard and I can just see Peter's undercarriage below my top wing as we enter the loop. James and I are now gaining hand over fist as we approach the top of the loop, (our spacing in time is always the same but as our speed changes, our actual distance apart varies). I start throttling back, but too late – Peter's aircraft appears to rush towards me and in sudden fright I bang the throttle shut. Peter's tailplane hovers between my wing tips and I am aware of a baleful eye glaring at me – I can just imagine the language in his cockpit! This one time I'm glad we have no radios! My ailerons still roll the aircraft, but as the 'g' drops towards zero and the lift falls off, there is no lift component available to enable me to turn away. At the same time I know that unless I open the throttle, I'm going to be left behind. James is still sitting there making it look easy, blast him! Well, it's now or never – full throttle and – I knew I'd left it too late; Peter starts to move ahead. A touch of rudder does the trick – I ease out a foot or so and I find I've been holding my breath! I crouch in the cockpit trying to coax an extra knot or so out of my aircraft; I glance across at James and am relieved to see he has the same problem. Peter meanwhile is throttling back as he knows that we could never catch him on the way down otherwise. This is no time for finesse; again I throttle back and at the same time I can see James's prop slow down. As we approach level flight, I know that Peter is going to increase power and in anticipation I start opening the throttle. We're still pulling about 4 'g' and I for one have had enough for one afternoon!

Thank God for that, straight and level and we're still in formation! Well, I might have known it was too good to last; Peter is signalling wing-over right. This is a manoeuvre I detest, being on the outside, as I don't have any power to spare. As he signals I open throttle wide – this makes an appreciable difference as our drag is so high at this speed (120 knots). Sure enough I start to fall behind. Cheating furiously I edge in closer and drop down hoping that Peter will notice my problem and throttle back a bit. James on the inside of the wing-over just grins – he's got plenty to spare! Life gets easier as we exceed 45° bank and the difference in the radius of turn starts decreasing again. As I finally get into position Peter signals "straight ahead" and indicates a second loop. We roll out and this time it's James's turn to sweat as he swings up from the inside with his throttle wide open. That'll teach him to grin, I think, gaining in turn. The loop goes OK until we reach the top and James and I virtually fall across the top, both bank away from Peter and both unable to increase our separation. We have a choice here: either we pull back hard at which point the wings will start doing a job of work again or we sit here with our eyes closed and our fingers in our ears hoping for the best. James appears to be sticking it out and so I decide to do likewise. Later I find out that he's been waiting for me to break away. Peter twigs the problem and pulls tighter and we heave a sigh of relief as control returns. This time we already have full power on, and we cut the corner slightly to catch Peter on the way down. Another wing-over this time to the left and I'm looking straight up at two Tigers apparently hanging in space. This is impossible, I think, they're bound to fall on top of me. I have to concentrate hard to try to fly steadily and not cross my controls. It occurs to me that James doesn't appear to be having any trouble on the outside!

I still haven't seen the crowd yet. I suppose we're still over an airfield! Well, that's Peter's problem, I've got enough trouble! Yet a third loop, wonder of wonders, no complications. Why can't we do them like that all the time?

A steep turn to the right – and there's the crowd, we're in the right place! Not that there was any chance that we wouldn't be, but it's nice to see them anyway. I wake up with a start as I realise that Peter is signalling to me. He points at me and waves his arm across to the right – echelon starboard – go! I throttle back a touch, drop down and put on about 30° of bank – this change is going to be snappy. As I slide across behind James, my port wing tips encounter his slipstream and I find myself straight and level much too soon, well stepped down and too far in. I slink furtively into position, hoping nobody will notice. My neck is stiff from looking constantly to the right; it's a pleasant change to turn my head the other way. I am startled at the sudden appearance of a Tiger Moth in plain view, which disappears instantly as Peter breaks hard. Start counting – one – two – three and James goes after him – four – five – six and I open the throttle wide and apply full aileron.

Below and ahead I can see James diving while ahead of him Peter is curving round the field, his yellow and black machine contrasting sharply with the green countryside. I suddenly feel very small as I look around; after five minutes formation one tends to forget the existence of the ground, the airfield and the hangars, and the only real objects are the aircraft in the formation. It's akin to walking along a cliff and coming suddenly to the edge. I can't recommend that for a pastime either!

But to work! Peter appears to be trying to get on my tail, while I am desperately trying not to lose James. At the back of this follow-my-leader, I have two slipstreams to contend with, and I spend most of my time trying to prevent my aircraft from indulging in a series of flick rolls. Finally we run out of altitude and Peter rocks his wings. At full throttle we join up and sure enough we tend to overcook it. Peter, however, is watching and opens his throttle to prevent us shooting past. Into a steep turn to the left – oh, when is this going to stop? I am soaked in perspiration – yes, even in a Tiger and my arms and legs are aching.... I force myself to relax my vice-like grip on the control column and to uncurl my toes from the rudder bar. Peter signals a 'Prince of Wales' as we enter a dive and we nod our understanding. This is one of the most exciting parts of the whole display as we sweep across the field only a few feet up. Peter starts to pull up as James breaks and I go with him. As I near the completion of my chandelle to the left, I look across at James and attempt to maintain the same height. I am aware of Peter completing a roll off the top between us. As he finishes he dives to his right beneath me and I see James start to follow him down. At the same time I go into a 270° turn to the left, relaxed for the first time since now the actual formation is complete. James is dead ahead as I roll out and we turn round the field and finish with a good low beat-up in line astern. I make sure that I stay well away from slipstream at this height! We pull up individually into stall turns and then it's every man for himself as we slip in for the landing.

Peter walks across as James and I climb out of our Tigers discussing the finer points of the loops. “That change into echelon was a bit ragged”, he says.

The very last Touring Air Show

This tale by Lewis Benjamin gives some of the background to what became known as the Caithness Saga (see below the story by James Gilbert). Neil Williams also wrote his story of the Saga and published it in his book 'Airborne' under the heading 'A Tiger to the Rescue'.

Once upon a time, well, that's how legends are supposed to begin, there was a farmer who lived with his lovely daughter right up north where Scotland drops into the sea at a town called Thurso. Anyway this farmer flew south in the spring of 1963, saw a Tiger Club airshow, was hugely impressed and invited the team back as his guests and so give his neighbours the sight of a live performance, something that hadn't been seen up there since before the war when Alan Cobham had once turned up and so began an extraordinary adventure.

The Tiger Club then was a thriving pilot outfit whose main joy was giving airshows. Not for money, at the best we got our expenses, because that we relished the skills needed, it gave our flying a sense of purpose. All our displays were in house, our members tackled every task.

In May of 63 Bill Chesson and I flew north in the Jodel D117 to set things up. Bill to take on the organising bit, I to eyeball fields to land in, mindful that a 600 mile journey would be no small undertaking given that our average speed would be around 55 knots – two days worth of hard open air flying sans radio.

From an historic point of view, I doubt whether light aviation will ever again see another 8 ship balbo of club aircraft – volunteers all – sally forth so far in search of an audience, or in doing so risk so much for so little. But then we started out in innocence.

We finally set sail for Thurso (Castletown) after an airshow we had given that Easter Monday at Sywell, Northants, into the growing dusk to RAF Middleton St. George near Newcastle for our night stay courtesy of the Wingco flying John Severne. Before we set off the next day we put on a bit of an impromptu show. The sight of my wife Lollie waving on top of Tiger RAZ made a nice change from the resident Lightnings.

The ten green bottles had nothing on us. James Gilbert couldn't start his Turbulent. Arthur Humphreys also Turb mounted and Don and Tessa Lovell in the Jodel Ambassadeur stayed to keep him company. James Baring in the third Turbulent had already dropped into Tollerton with a busted oil pipe. Not half way there already four down.

The three biplanes, two Tigers and a Stampe, flew on across the Highlands in beautiful evening sunshine alternatively slope soaring, then hugging the base of the cu-nim that lay across the peaks in an endeavour to conserve fuel. Above us Bill in the Jodel D140 was mother hen.

Nearly out of fuel we dropped into a deserted field. A tractor arrived and the farmer asked if it would be OK to pump fuel. Fussy we weren't. We left behind a gathering of some fifty cheerful locals who waved us on our way.

Castletown proved to be a fine surfaced disused airfield right on the coast in clear view of the Orkneys and edged by the bluest sea outside the Med. The hospitality was red carpet. On Wednesday afternoon the three Turbs flew over in tight formation shepherded by the faithful Ambassadeur. We were back to strength.

Two airshows had been planned both in the evening at seven. At ten to seven a vast fog bank swept in. The base hung around at 100 feet. Total clamp happened again the next night. Rather than disappoint again we put on a show. Spectacular wasn't in it. Nick Pocock's forte was really low knife edge four point rolls in the Stampe. Not to be outdone Neil Williams climbed in and did his inverted runs nearly ploughing up the earth. Formations turned with a number two in cloud and standing on wing was remarkable for a vision of two legs standing on an aeroplane. It was unrepeatable madness. The locals cheered.

Later that evening after a fine meal James Baring, bewitched by the drink and the stars decided to walk the twenty miles back to our hosts for breakfast. Knackered and flaked out. A while later two evangelists called by. Ever helpful, Neil suggested they might find a hungover sinner upstairs. All listened with glee as they were noisily ejected. Shaken, they were unanimous that no way was the gentleman ever likely to se the light.

Then everything went to pot. Horace Henderson, our genial host, urged us to stay to give our show on Saturday afternoon. But Lollie and I couldn't stay on. After two abortive attempts on the Thursday and Friday to put on a show, we had to resist the entreaties of our friends. It wasn't easy but we *had* to be back in London on the Monday.

Farewells, and we turned Tiger RAZ into wind at Castletown and hurried back to Thurso and the little harbour to dip our wings in salute and then head towards Inverness. Above us around 1500 feet a solid layer of cloud hung darkly. After a while we left the comfort of the solitary Thurso road and climbed steadily to the plateau between the twin peaks of the Caithness range. We slipped through, skirting the cloud, and sank thankfully down to the coast. Across Dornoch Firth bucking the wind at a cheerful 200 feet to speed across the lowlands towards the airport at Inverness. Cloud base 1000 feet.

Tea, refuel and a word with the controller. He phoned Aberdeen. To make Perth was out. The rest of Scotland lay beneath a mantle of fog. Only the coast was clear. Aberdeen weather was down to two miles and a cloud base of 800 feet. We consulted the map and reckoned that, provided we followed the Moray coast and only moved inland beyond Elgin, we'd miss the high ground. It was a try anyway. We could always return. It was dank and chilly, Aberdeen was on our way and anyway it might not be as bad as forecast.

Up past Lossiemouth with the viz dropping we left the coast to edge inland. No longer the clean definition of cloud and land. Instinctively I wiped my hand across the lenses of my goggles and followed the lowly Aberdeen road. A lorry driver waved. His wipers were busy, the road glistened. I hadn't realised I was so low. The misty drizzle had suddenly reduced our little world to that road and the hills which rose steeply either side of us. The map clearly showed the valley and the big plain beyond it. Too late to turn back and with the stark knowledge that we either scraped through or we were going to have to climb through with the certainty of 8/8th cover beneath us. Viz had nearly gone. The rain beat on my face. I glued my attention to that road and then, suddenly, we were through. Now the road led us to the railway – the very railway which actually crossed the edge of the runway. All I had to do now was to stay with it. Every sense said: 'You were lucky, don't push it, get down, make a precautionary, the weather is worsening'. But the roar of the engine, the sureness of our position, and with the knowledge that the airport wasn't nine minutes away weakened my senses.

Just a little further – decide then. And then it was too late. Imperceptibly the rain, the cloud and the fog became one. Impossible now to lob in anywhere. All that was visible was a hazy railway track 80 feet below. Nothing else showed, not even the fields either side, just the wet blinding fog. The marshalling yards and no more than a mile to go – HT cables, a heave back into the mire and push down the other side. Blindly searching for the runway. A chimney passed. Too late to worry. A huge white numeral; that's all we saw, not even the edges of the runway.

They were a nice crowd at Aberdeen. No fuss. "Didn't see you", they said. "Let's get your Tiger into a hangar".

Stampes in Grande Bretagne - Early Days

The first Stampe to land permanently in Britain was the famous SV4B purloined from a shed in the grounds of a Belgian chateau in 1941 and flown across the North Sea under cover of darkness and the noses of the Luftwaffe by two young Belgian pilots. Both the Stampe OO-ATD and the pilots were impressed into the RAF and the aircraft was eventually restored to its legal owner in 1945. Michael Jones continues the history:

One of the curious facts about the Stampe is that it was not until 1962 that the first one arrived on the British register. Most of the Stampes built in France and later in Algeria were 'sortie d'usine' between 1945 and 1950 and production of SV4Bs finished in Belgium in 1955. Apart from the import restrictions on light aircraft which existed pre-1958 probably the main reason was the easy availability of the ubiquitous Tiger Moth at ridiculously low prices. In the end it was aerobatics which brought the Stampe to Britain.

Stampes flown by French pilots had successfully competed in the Lockheed Trophy since 1955. British pilots from the Tiger Club struggled manfully to match the Stampe with the Rollason Super Tiger but it was not until that somebody suggested that the only thing to do to the Super Tiger was to fit a second pair of ailerons to the top wing like the Stampe, that Neil Williams came up with the rather better idea that it would be quicker and easier to acquire a Stampe! Consequently Neil was instructed by the Tiger Club committee to locate a good second hand SV4C and deliver it as soon as possible to Redhill. As a result G-AROZ arrived from Lognes in late 1961 with a clapped out Renault engine.

The aircraft was converted to the Gipsy Major during the winter by Rollasons and given a complete overhaul including the familiar red and yellow colour scheme. It was fully ready and prepared for the Lockheed Trophy in 1962 when it was flown into third place by Peter Phillips, beating all but one of the French Stampe pilots who were all flying SV4Cs.

After its rebuild G-AROZ was christened by the Tiger Club, the 'Leon Biancotto' not only in memory of a brilliant aerobatic pilot but also in recognition of the fact that this same pilot had sportingly competed the year before in the Lockheed in a Super Tiger and had achieved a remarkable fourth place. The postscript to the G-AROZ story was provided by Neil Williams at the Biggin Hill Air Fair in 1965; the aircraft failed to recover from a flick roll at low altitude and was completely wrecked. Neil emerged unscathed and always the perfectionist puzzled for a long time over this unfortunate lapse. What was left of the wreckage was removed to Farnborough, where Neil worked as a test pilot, and the conclusion was eventually reached that the C of G had moved fractionally aft as a result of an extra coat of paint applied to the tailplane on the aircraft's last overhaul. (Neil's account of this accident is contained in his book 'Airborne').

The next two Stampes to arrive on the British register were G-ASHS and G-ATKC. I had the pleasure of flying G-ASHS from Lognes during a bitterly cold January in 1963. Fortunately on the first leg to Toussus to clear customs, I had the services of a French 'moniteur' who gave me a very detailed briefing on the intricacies of starting the Renault in cold weather. The aircraft was in good condition and was kept for the first year by the Tiger Club in its SV4C configuration, its Renault engine surviving the attention of the Club's rapidly growing aerobatic contingent. G-ATKC was flown by Neil from Dinard in 1965 and both aircraft were given the Rollason treatment and conversion to SV4Bs for the 1965 season.

There is no doubt that the arrival of 'SHS' and 'TKC' at the Tiger Club was the beginning of an enduring love affair with the Stampe by a great many British sporting pilots and not only aerobatic aficionados. The late 1960s saw the trickle of arrivals from across the Channel turn into a minor flood. Other enterprises apart from Rollasons entered the market encouraged no doubt by the sponsorship of a Stampe aerobatic team by Rothmans, the cigarette manufacturer. Incidentally the Rothmans MD in Asia was a little known member of the Tiger Club who never actually flew the Stampe but according to Manx Kelly who founded the team he said: "Don't bother me with the details. Just tell me how much you need"!

Rollason's policy at the time was to fetch Stampes by road preferably without their Renault engines but I did get involved with an expedition in December 1966 which sticks in the memory. The objective was to fetch a Stampe from the Club airfield at Lille and deliver it to Redhill in the course of a single day. I was organising the trip with an Australian member of the Tiger Club, David Allan, who was on a very extended holiday from his family business in Melbourne. Anyway we duly picked up the Stampe from the small grass airfield at Lille after only a short delay and proceeded to the main airport for customs clearance with me shepherding the Stampe in a Jodel. One of the lessons I had learnt from collecting Jodels from Bernay on short winter days was that it was absolutely necessary to clear the paperwork in France before lunch if one was not eventually to run out of daylight on the flight home particularly as the customs at Lympne had a habit of closing in mid-afternoon.

To cut a long story short, the customs at Lille had gone to lunch by the time we arrived and after lunch we were told that the 'chef' was not back and the process of exporting a Stampe from France was too complicated for mere juniors. As the minutes ticked by and deadlines came and went our exasperation grew in direct proportion to the 'insouciance' displayed by minor French officialdom. Already David and I had agreed that he would have to fly direct to Redhill to avoid being trapped by darkness and even this course was now being threatened. Soon we decided that the Stampe would have to leave regardless and we proceeded to the apron outside the terminal building to start up. As soon as it dawned on the 'douaniers', that a departure was imminent – the Stampe incidentally did not have the benefit of radio – two fire engines raced to erect a 'barrage' on the runway. David, meanwhile, realising what was happening, quick as a flash, opened the throttle and took off on the empty tarmac outside the terminal. Some minutes later I started up the Jodel for a pre-arranged departure to Toussus and was surprised to receive a formal clearance albeit in somewhat icy tones. The Stampe duly arrived at Redhill and poor David was later fined by HM Customs for failing to enter the United Kingdom at a properly authorised Customs airport. We heard nothing from the French authorities; their customs paperwork was later cleared over the phone by my colleague at Rollasons, Frank Hounslow, who spoke fluent French. I expect that the file was marked 'force majeure'. Anyway that was how the Stampe later to become G-AWEF first arrived in Britain.

Rollasons imported some 14 Stampes between 1962 and 1972; not all of them were restored completely to airworthy condition since one or two were cannibalised to repair those broken in accidents. In 1970 Rollasons negotiated the manufacturing rights and the purchase of a large quantity of spare parts from the old Stampe and Renard production line in Belgium. In 1971 the company was offering completely re-built SV4Bs with full inverted systems and nil hour engines for £3900.

According to Stampe historian Reginald Jouhaud in 1992 there were 65 Stampes on the British register and no doubt to-day there are quite a few more although there is some evidence that the French are getting a little worried by the numbers which are leaving France. It was not very long ago that the Tiger Club sold its last remaining Stampe, G-AWEF, to a Club member to be replaced by a CAP 10. The interests of Stampe owners in the UK continue to be well looked after by the British Stampe Club and there are similar organisations in Belgium and France. Despite alarms and accidents – two tragic – Stampes served the Tiger Club marvellously well for more than forty years and they were unrivalled in the fields of competition aerobatics, displays and for sheer flying enjoyment.

Accidents and Incidents

The Tiger Club had strict rules for reporting accidents and incidents to the Club Committee and what follows made a particular impression on Michael Jones. The incident referred to also featured in Neil Williams' book 'Airborne'.

'It is with regret that I have to report the loss of Stampe SV4B G-AVCO whilst under my command at Redhill at approximately 15.45 hours local time on Saturday 8th June 1968'. The statement to the Chairman and Committee was plain enough and the pilot had little else to say except that he was practising an advanced aerobatic manoeuvre in the hope that he might eventually be considered for the British team for the World Aerobatic Championships to be held at Magdeburg later that year. The accident was memorable and traumatic for me not only because I had witnessed it but also the day before I had been contemplating with trepidation the prospect of extracting G-AVCO from a school playing field in far off west Wales.

G-AVCO, a recent addition to the Club's Stampe fleet from Rollasons, had been due back from a display in Ireland the week before. However I had received a phone call from Neil Williams that the engine had started to run rough over the Irish Sea and he had just made the coast in time to make a precautionary landing in a school playing field at Pendine. "It was no problem", said Neil, "the headmaster has promised to look after the aircraft and the local police are quite happy. It is almost certainly a cracked cylinder head. I hope you can fix it and get the aircraft back to Redhill in time for the Saturday afternoon practice". As he gave me the details, Neil spoke in his usual clipped and confident manner and there was a note of satisfaction in his voice. It did not take long to organise another Gipsy Major cylinder head from the Rollason engine shop at Croydon and also an engineer, Reg Johns, another committed Welshman, who relished the prospect of spending a week-end in the land of his fathers and fixing a Gipsy Major in trouble.

So armed with overnight bags, a cylinder head, gaskets and a set of tools we caught the early morning train from Paddington to arrive at Carmarthen in the late morning. I forget how we got from Carmarthen to Pendine but when we arrived at the playing field, the Stampe was fine, well picketed down, and the school authorities were delighted to see us. However while Reg set to work to replace the cylinder head, I was examining the playing field in some dismay. I don't know what it is about school playing fields; I have often thought that, in theory, they make ideal landing grounds for light aircraft because they are both flat and smooth, but they do need to be large enough. The one at Pendine was decidedly on the small side and I wondered how on earth Neil managed to get the Stampe in there undamaged. I was also reflecting on the time when Clive Francis, an RAF squadron leader and enthusiastic boss of the Club's Turbulent team had been appointed by the Air Ministry to the job of schools liaison officer. He had received permission from his superiors to use a Club Turbulent for his liaison visits to various schools up and down the country. Clive had told me that at one or two schools he had had some really hair raising moments and now I hoped that I was not going to make a fool of myself in G-AVCO on the school cricket ground at Pendine in front of a gathering crowd.

But as it turned out, all was well. Reg made short work of fixing the engine. There was a brisk westerly wind blowing down the take-off path and G.AVCO sailed happily into the air just clearing some tennis courts, after a brief stop at Swansea for fuel, the rest of the flight back home was uneventful and I thought I could relax!

But the next afternoon – Saturday – I was sitting in the cockpit of a Jodel outside the hangar facing south giving a briefing to a member before a type check flight. Aerobatic practice was in full swing and G-AVCO was much in demand. I happened to glance up. There was G-AVCO spinning earthwards in an attitude which was looking horribly flat! I am not an expert myself but frankly the manoeuvre that initiated this spectacle was immaterial. It was obvious that recovery would be difficult if not impossible in the height available and while G-AVCO was disappearing behind some trees on the south side of the aerodrome I rushed to the telephone fearing the worst. Meanwhile others hurtled across the aerodrome in the Landrover, leapt over a ditch to see poor G-AVCO spread-eagled in a field but also, mercifully, the pilot, wearing a bone dome, extricating himself from the wreckage comparatively unscathed. A recovery of sorts had been made!

The accident and the incident the week before were soon forgotten. True Neil Williams wrote an angry letter to the Committee. Neil's authority on all aerobatic matters was never questioned; he emphasised that the front cockpit of the Stampe should always be faired in and the front windscreen removed before any serious aerobatic practice, he disagreed that bone domes were necessarily a good idea for pilots in open cockpit aircraft; 'the object', wrote Neil, 'was to prevent accidents rather than to accept that one is inevitable' and among several other points he demanded that all aerobatic pilot members should be checked at least once a month on spin recovery both erect and inverted.

G-AVCO was, of course, eventually rebuilt by Rollasons but the machine never did rejoin G-ASHS and G-ATKC to make up the Club trio of Stampes since later in 1968 G-AWEF arrived! Much later G-AVCO was acquired by an enthusiastic Australian member from another owner and given the registration VH-WEF. The last we heard was that it had been seriously damaged following engine trouble and a forced landing in a swamp at Wagga Wagga.

The Arrival of the Cosmic Wind

It was during a visit to that delightful grass airfield – Eggington – to look at the Martin Jones Beta under construction that the conversation idly turned to the Cosmic Wind and to the Ballerina in particular. Martin told Michael Jones that there is a project under way to build a batch of Cosmic Winds and that the plans, material and tooling was still available. It will be remembered that the Ballerina II was built by Paul Bannister after the original Ballerina crashed at Halfpenny Green in 1966 during a handicap air race. Ballerina I1 has had several owners and has cleaned up several Formula I air races in Europe and is currently safely in the hands of Peter Kynsey and based at Duxford.

The original Ballerina was built in 1947 to compete in the annual Goodyear and Continental Motor 190 cubic inch pylon races held in the USA. She was the third of a batch of three, the other two being Little Toni and Minnow. The type was designated officially as the Le Vier Cosmic Wind but unofficially was designed and built by Lockheed and benefited from highly professional engineering, immense strength, superb aerodynamics and remarkable handling qualities and all on a Continental C85 engine.

The Ballerina G-ARUL (N22C) arrived at Redhill and the Tiger Club at the end of 1961 and for the next five years played a very important part in the life of the Club. Although she scored a Kings Cup victory and essentially was the inspiration for the British Formula 1 racing movement which came several years later with the arrival of Betas and Cassutts, it was not as a racer but as an airshow star and aerobatic mount that Ballerina made her mark at the Tiger Club. In fact as far as aerobatics were concerned the performance of the machine on 85 HP was a sensation and soon some of the Club's AF members were comparing the aircraft to a military jet. Remember that the high powered Pitts Specials and its successors were not yet on the scene. The Ballerina was capable of some extraordinary and original manoeuvres and selected Club members notably Peter Phillips and Neil Williams were soon competing for display slots in the Club airshows. In fact Neil became so enamoured with the Ballerina that he determined to enter her for the World Aerobatic Championships which were to take place at Bilbao in 1964 and he actually received financial support from the RAF to do so. As it turned out, despite the limitations of an extremely rudimentary inverted fuel system he achieved a very commendable result. All of this may be familiar to readers of Neil's book – 'airborne'- but some people may not know how the Tiger Club had the good fortune to acquire the Cosmic Wind 'Ballerina' in the first place. So here is the story:

It was on a gloomy November day in 1961 that news came through to the Tiger Club at Redhill: a tall American and his girl friend had arrived at Southampton docks with a car and a trailer towing a tiny but extremely pretty green monoplane. He had asked the way to the nearest airport which was Eastleigh. There he had assembled the machine before a gathering crowd. He had then proceeded on the aircraft's first take-off to perform two aileron rolls in rapid succession followed by a display of aerobatics the like of which had never been seen before on such a small aeroplane. The American was Milton C. Blair. It was said that he was a Texan; in fact he had an address in California. But Texan or Californian Milton Blair might have stepped strait off the set of a Hollywood western – colourful, extrovert with an explosive temperament, undoubtedly he would have been extremely quick on the draw! The tiny monoplane was, of course, one of the mythical Cosmic Winds which had not been heard of for at least ten years.

As luck would have it, one of the onlookers at Eastleigh had been Bill Chesson, the Club's display promoter. Eastleigh was one of the Club's regular display venues and he had probably been talking to the owner about the 1962 event. Bill immediately recognised the display potential of the Ballerina and he knew that the Club had the pilots to exploit it. Immediately he did two things: he advised Milton Blair that, if it was his intention to sell the midget racer, to fly it to Redhill without further delay and, secondly, he telephoned the Club's Chairman, Norman Jones, to say that if he acquired the aircraft for the Club it would be an extremely sound investment! Consequently a few days later the Ballerina arrived at Redhill after a brief stop at Lasham where Milton not only checked his navigation but also put on a further aerobatic display. Milton and his girlfriend then, spurning local hostelleries, installed themselves in the first floor of the control tower at Redhill where the Club had a makeshift club-room while the aircraft was lodged in the hangar to be examined minutely and admired by all and sundry. After Blair had put on further demonstrations, two or three Club members were allowed to sample the aircraft and one of his stock remarks to the privileged few after taxiing back to the hangar after a sortie was: "Go on, admit it! It was better than sex"!

Negotiations with Norman Jones over the purchase of the Ballerina did not go smoothly particularly on a personal level. Norman was suspicious that Milton Blair might not have legal title to the aircraft. Also he instinctively distrusted at the time anything that was not made of wood and fabric unless it had been manufactured by De Havillands! His company, Rollasons, had no expertise in all metal airframes and he wanted to know if there were any drawings or plans if the Cosmic Wind were to be damaged. He was also instinctively suspicious of the Ballerina's unique scimitar metal prop. Would it be possible to get a replacement if it were broken? Although Milton was asking a price which was a good deal more than Norman was willing to pay, he took particularly umbrage at many of these questions and he had to be calmed down after his meetings with Norman. Fortunately Bill Chesson got in touch with the FAA who confirmed that Milton C Blair was indeed the legal owner of the Ballerina. But Norman was right to be worried about the prop. Many years later the owner of Little Toni which was sold to another air racing enthusiast informed the Club that the scimitar metal props used on racing aircraft in the USA had been withdrawn from use since most of them had failed fatigue crack tests. The one on the Ballerina led a charmed life despite having to be straitened once. It was the secret of the machines impressive performance at full throttle since through a twisting action it stopped the engine from overrevving.

Eventually much to everyone's relief a document was signed that in theory covered most of Norman's worries and the Ballerina changed hands for £3200. Left out of the deal was the trailer and the ferry tank which could be installed behind the pilot's seat with a change over fuel cock in the cockpit. The fuel system was gravity fed and Milton Blair advised that the pilot would 'buy the farm' if the main tank was used up while the ferry tank remained full. Incidentally 'buying the farm' was one of Milton's favourite expressions! So the Cosmic Wind joined the Arrow Active in 1962 on the Club's list of flying rates as a restricted type at £9.00 per hour (The Tiger Moth at the time was £3.00 per hour) and it was agreed that if the aircraft was used on displays an extra £150 would be asked.

After the cheque was cashed Milton Blair and his girl friend left Redhill never to return. Some considerable time later it was learnt that he had been killed in Paul Bannister's Midget Mustang following an engine failure on take-off. However during 1962 there was a sequel to the Club's deal with Milton Blair. A letter was received from Her Majesty's Customs and Excise at Southampton containing a newspaper cutting. It was apparent that Milton had told a local journalist at Eastleigh that the aircraft had been built by Lockheed's and had cost 'hundreds and thousands of dollars'. On arrival at Southampton docks he had declared it as a model aircraft and had paid a trifling sum in duty. Since Norman Jones was now the legal owner he was liable for the extra duty at a valuation to be agreed with Customs and Excise. Although a considerable sum was due, it was paid up cheerfully. By that time the little lady had demonstrated that she was well worth the price!

An Easter Monday

Neil Williams' commentary on his own display of the Cosmic Wind 'Ballerina' is well known and no collection of tales from the Tiger Rag would be complete without it:

"....What a hell of a way to spend Easter Monday! So run my thoughts as I strip off my heavier flying kit and, considerably lightened, sprint across to the 'Ballerina'. Tony has the canopy open and the straps laid out ready. Thoroughly out of breath I scramble aboard, cursing all displays, directors and close time schedules. A glance at my watch – eight minutes past four; my display starts in nine minutes time. What if the engine won't start?

I force myself to concentrate on strapping in; if Tony can't start it I'll eat my helmet! Lap straps first – tight! Can't afford any loose movement there, shoulder harness tight, that b.... parachute box is crippling me; I'll have to move it – ten past four – no, damn it! I haven't got time. Switches off, throttle closed, cold air, cylinder head temperature selected to no. 2 – set, contact. My legs are trembling as I hold the toe brakes on – still on, from Tony – my god! It isn't going to start. No sooner than the thought than she fires and I just grab the canopy in time as the slipstream tries to slam it down. I close it and slide the bolts home, oil pressure ok, oil temperature 25°C, eleven minutes past four;

I check the stopwatch on the panel and set the altimeter to zero. Mags dead and alive and I wave the boys away, 1600 rpm and she rolls forward waggling her wings and giving me a resounding clout on the ear as she bumps over the grass. Checks as I taxi and make a rude sign at John Blake. He says something into the mike equally rude no doubt but I can't hear anything inside this flying echo chamber.

Twelve minutes past four – five minutes to go, never thought I'd make it, must complain to Benjy, extra heave on the harness adjusting straps and we are ready to go. Two Turbulent formations are running in, I'll have to wait, God! This cloud looks low. I tie loose strap ends together, mustn't have those in my face during the display. The Turbs cross and I open up to 2000 rpm, check mags full power and we gallop. Airborne, just behind the Turbs, turn away, keep it low clear of the field, phew! Airspeed 130 into the climb and run through the pre-aerobatic checks – hullo, cloud base 1500 – not so good, still there are breaks, and I climb in a gentle spiral, 3000 feet in the clear, but it's a pretty small hole I came up through. A couple of rolls to make sure the harness is really tight and to check for loose articles – two minutes to go, I'd better get into position, throttle back, the slipstream whines mournfully round the canopy as I break out beneath the – where the hell is the airfield?! It can't be far away – 90 seconds to go – how I am going to explain this away? Turn into the wind, fingers crossed, a wave of relief, there it is, what a devil of a place to try and find, even then I could only see the crowd – 60 seconds and I'm right out of position, full throttle. Come on airspeed, 150, 160, 170, the staccato engine note changes into a blare of sound – the noise is terrific, 30 seconds to run and I pull up into cloud – ease forward, needle in the centre and down we go. 1800 feet, 1600 – 1500 and the airfield is dead ahead

– airspeed 190 and increasing. A wave of fright – the sky is full of Turbulents! What the hell are they playing at?

I must have got the time wrong. Shall I keep going, shall I break off – airspeed 210 – height 1000 feet – too late, I am committed, check my watch, five seconds to go, the noise is devastating, airspeed check 230, the crowd changes from a coloured rectangle to a sea of upturned faces, she's snaking now very sensitive on the rudder, clamp those pedals hard, throttle back a bit, the revs nearly off the clock, bang the stopwatch – start pulling, airspeed 240, brace hard against the lap belt, she's really moving, the nose is up, my breath comes in gasps as the 'g' builds up, vertical, full power, the 'g' is very high now as the horizon comes in – push!

Plus 9 to minus 4 as we go into the second half of the 'S', the engine cuts, bang the throttle shut, keep pushing and she comes over the top at 50 indicated. There is fuel everywhere; it's streaming out of the filler cap. I can't see ahead, the windscreen is running with it, the cockpit is thick with petrol fumes, I hope none gets into the exhaust pipes – the prop is slowing, it's going to stop, ease back on the stick gently. She judders on the stall but I get in a quick pump on the throttle which helps me over the top with a sudden burst of power. The engine cuts again but now the nose is down, 70 knots (the straight and level stalling speed) 80, 90 – vertical. God, that ground looks close but whatever you do don't push or she'll stall inverted, 120, 130 and push gently, she's coming round, that ground looks desperately close, gently does it, the negative 'g' is up to 4 and the nose is on the horizon. I roll as smoothly as I can to go to straight and level flight – 400 feet, plenty of room actually. So the show goes on for another terrifying four and half minutes, flying the aeroplane to its limits, knowing that every mistake is recognised by fellow pilots

– this to me is the biggest ordeal. Nearly over – a wingover into ten successive aileron rolls – if this one doesn't topple your gyros nothing will! I level out for a fraction and then go into a tight turn – this is because I am so dizzy that I couldn't fly straight and level if I wanted to!

Relax, boy, this is the final manoeuvre, right on the deck, full power, airspeed 170 that is plenty. Keep it going as the centre of the crowd comes up a quick check on the stopwatch again, it shows fifteen seconds to go – that's about right, pull up at about 7 'g' and check vertical (and if anyone thinks I'm going to tell them how I do a lomcevak they have had it!). As the rotation stops I pull out of the dive and bang the throttle shut. With the engine popping and banging I pull up and round into the downwind leg as the sailplane releases high above me. All attention is on the quiet grace of the glider as I cross the threshold and ease down on to the grass.

I switch off and open the canopy, sweating, deafened and completely exhausted. "Quick", says someone, "you've just got time to get into OAA, we've kept the engine running!" As I said before – what a hell of a way to spend an Easter Monday!

A Turbulent Story

Barry Griffiths, a London solicitor, was one of a small group of Tiger Club members who owned their own Rollason Turbulents in the 1960s. Most of these members had tales to tell and this story is one of the best:

This story is about an aeroplane – to the everlasting credit of that aeroplane. If it reflects rather less credit upon the pilot, I still think that it should be told for reasons which will appear.

It is a short story. It would have been longer, but after two thousand words, when I was half way through, I rang the editor, who said fifteen hundred at most, so I will leave out the exciting bits about how I got lost in the murk over France and shouted: "The blasted coast must be there". Only there was no answer and it wasn't.

I had started out in my Turbulent for the Beauvais thrash in company with assorted Club aircraft crammed with dedicated aviators, licking their lips in anticipation of the orgy to come, but the beasts pushed off and left me flogging along on my own, which I didn't really mind, as I didn't have to worry about keeping them in sight and after all we private owners must draw the line somewhere.

Now there those, I regret to say, who regard Turbulents as underpowered, unreliable, fragile and generally unfit to be taken out of sight of the aerodrome. It is to these dribbly-nosed beasts (if I may be forgiven a technicality) that this story is directed. To the rest may it confirm their faith.

Late on a Saturday afternoon I found myself and my Turbulent sitting in a field on a French farm. The field was 150 metres long with a barbed wire fence at each end; it had been formed when the earth was in torment – it was not a smooth field, you understand. I know that you would love to hear the gripping story of how I came to be there in the first place, the excitement, terror and pathos of it all. But it will cost you a drink to hear it. After a thrilling battle with the cows – who bitterly resented the intrusion – some rough but effective men chased them away and got me some petrol from a garage.

It had been difficult to get into that field, so any attempt to get out of it seemed to me quite hopeless; however my new friends were so obviously looking forward to seeing me try (they had brought with the petrol some village children to see me fail) that it seemed churlish to refuse. Furthermore the alternative was the dismantling of the aircraft (for no-one but a desperate owner would try to fly it out), endless explanations and colossal expense. If I could just get the wheels over that fence I could get to Le Treport before dark and the whole picture would change.

What wind there was came out of the sun. There were also some trees. With my heart in my mouth I started the engine, strapped myself in and taxied back down the abominable field. Four times I rushed up that field with the sun in my eyes dodging the cows as they loomed up; the poor little Turbulent bounced and rattled over the tussocks like a drunk, but the wheels would not unstuck and with never more than 20 on the clock, each time I had to slew violently away as the fence came up in front of the nose. I could not understand how the undercarriage was still in one piece but it was. I determined that the next attempt would decide the matter one way or the other. As the fence came into view a few feet ahead I dragged back on the stick and – glory be – there was air beneath the wheels. Wallowing impossibly I thought I had just scraped over when there was a bang and down came the Turbulent on her nose in the next field. I had acquired thirty feet of barbed wire, lost a spat, the pitot head and some fabric. This really did seem to be the end but we were in soft earth, the prop was whole and the engine started. The little lads were clearly delighted with this performance and willingly helped me manhandle the Turbulent through the mud. They pointed to some stubble some distance away and said it was 'plus dur'. They were getting the point. "Plus long?" I asked. No doubt with pathetic eagerness. They shook their heads. "le meme. Cent cinquante metres". Oh! Well.

Then I taxied over a deeply rutted cart track for about 200 yards. When I got to the stubble, the wheels, incredibly, were still turning. I abandoned the negligible wind for the advantage of going down sun. Once more I opened the throttle, felt the wheels dragging in the soft earth, banged in and out of a sharp dip; still no feeling of buoyancy but here comes the fence, so here goes. Once more back on the stick; again that feeling as the Turbulent was dragged off the ground against all one had ever been taught. I didn't dare look at the fence but simply waited for the bang and braced myself for the crash. But nothing happened. I don't know what the speed was because I had no ASI. But – glory be – we were airborne again flopping about like a drunken duck, but flying. Nothing came off and I landed 15 minutes later at Le Treport where they took one look at my dishevelled mud covered clothes, another look at the aircraft and poured me a vast brandy. After a hectic interlude at Beauvais - incidentally I got there by car to a welcome I certainly didn't deserve – I flew the Turbulent back to Redhill the next day. Don Lovell, considerate as ever, hovered up sun of me in the Ambassadeur, just in case. But the Turbulent behaved beautifully and I have never crossed the Channel with more confidence. An aircraft that could stand up to such appalling treatment and still perform normally was, to say the least, to be relied on.

And that is the point of this story.

A Turbulent Sea Story

In the small club room at the back of the Tiger Club's hangar at Redhill there was a photograph on the wall of a Turbulent floating half submerged in the English Channel with the pilot sitting comfortably on the rear decking waving. It was a reminder that a Turbulent would survive a ditching if necessary. Michael Jones who witnessed the event takes up the story:

The Turbulent was registered G-APZZ and was owned by a popular Club member, Robin d'Erlanger. It was on a summer's day in 1964 that Frank Hounslow and I had been on a business trip to Bernay where the S.A.N. Jodel factory was situated. We had flown out on one day via Gatwick and Deauville and were returning the next day via Le Touquet and Lympne. We were using the Club's Jodel Ambassadeur G-ASAB. At some point during this excursion we met up with Robin and his Turbulent. I cannot remember whether it was at Bernay or Le Touquet but I do recall that Robin was worried about the performance of his engine and we agreed that we would escort him across the Channel from Le Touquet to Lympne. G-ASAB had the benefit of a 12 channel VHF with the right frequencies, a set which at the time was also manufactured at Bernay. I cannot remember the nature of Robin's concerns but Frank who was Rollason's expert on the Ardem engine spent some time examining it without finding anything amiss.

Although I have made countless Channel crossings in many different types of light aircraft and in many different conditions, I have never made one without that well-known sensation of nervousness in the pit of the stomach before taking off and that almost tangible feeling of relief and even of triumph when one crosses the coast the other side. As we filed our flight plans at Le Touquet I vaguely sensed that Robin was also nervous but he was far too modest person to show it. At the time there were two common options for crossing the Channel between Cap Gris Nez and Folkestone – one could be called the low route and the other the high. As we left the French coast I could see immediately that Robin had opted for the low route. There was a fresh westerly breeze and the little Turbulent seemed literally to be skimming the wave tops. Possibly Robin had in mind that well-known French maxim: "To conquer without risk is to triumph without glory"! Frank and I on the other hand had chosen the high route keeping G-APZZ well in view below us.

We had crossed the mid Channel point but we were still several miles from the English coast when suddenly it happened! I saw the Turbulent banking sharply and turning into wind and then what seemed like only a few seconds later it ditched. The tail rose into the air and for an agonising moment I thought that the aircraft must turn over but slowly the tail fell back and G-APZZ was left bobbing in the waves with the engine and the wings partially submerged. Then Frank and I were both very relieved to see that Robin had levered himself out of the cockpit and was perched on the rear decking with his feet on the seat. He was waving to us apologetically.

It was then that I prayed that the Radiostal VHF would be on form and as calmly as possible I called up Lympne to tell them that the Turbulent had ditched and please would they do something about it. There was a pregnant pause and the message was duly acknowledged. Next, only a very few minutes later, a twin engined Cessna appeared and joined us circling the scene. Then I was again considerably relieved to see that a nearby cargo ship, obviously attracted by the commotion above, had altered course and was heading for the spot. Then two other light aircraft one of which was a Tripacer also appeared seemingly from nowhere. The sky was now becoming uncomfortably overcrowded and when a Skyways DC3 on route from Lympne to Beauvais started to join the merry go round with its passengers gaping from the cabin windows in amazement, I thought it best to get out of the way before something else happened! Also we had noticed that the ship had launched a boat propelled by oars and was now beginning to effect a rescue. Finally I had overheard a message on the radio from the Cessna that it was returning to Lympne immediately in order to get the photos into the London evening papers before it was too late!

We landed at Lympne and learnt that an RAF air-sea rescue helicopter had arrived on the scene, had winched Robin from the deck of the ship and had taken him to Manston, also that his Turbulent had been recovered from the sea and was remaining on board while the ship continued on its voyage to some unknown port in Northern Europe. Later we flew to Manston to pick up Robin and there we were not only able to congratulate him on his sage return but also to confirm the story that he did not even get his feet wet !

Eventually the ship's owners claimed salvage on the Turbulent which was declared a write-off as far as its insurers were concerned. But a long time later a rumour was circulating amongst the home building fraternity that G-APZZ had been restored to health and was flying somewhere in West Germany. As for Robin d'Erlanger he did not buy another Turbulent but a Jodel of the Dijon variety instead.

Unusual Types

One of the attractions for members of the Tiger Club during the Redhill era was the occasional arrival in the hangar of various unusual flying machines – for one reason or another. Michael Jones whose job it was to manage the hangar has some memories:

Needless to say examples of many of the usual types were always there – several varieties of DH Moths, and even a Dove and Heron in the very early days, refugees from the closure of Croydon and of course all the many and various types operated by the Club including the single seaters which could always be squeezed in somewhere; in fact one day someone counted nineteen single seaters, mainly Turbulents and Formula 1 racers. Also Rollasons used the hangar to assemble all the aircraft they manufactured or rebuilt at Croydon.

Amongst this colourful array one or two very unusual aircraft sometimes found a space and they inevitably attracted large numbers of people from the aircraft spotters fraternity, in fact so much so that one day the owners of the airfield felt obliged to erect notices at every possible entrance: 'Aircraft Spotters Strictly Not Admitted', a notice which in my opinion was likely to encourage visitors rather than to put them off!

Some of these aircraft did not stay long; two arrived after epic long distance flights, a twin engined General Aircraft Monospar with Gipsy Majors from Australia and a Danish KZ III from Singapore. One known as a Pixie arrived on a trailer and it soon became apparent that the owner was trying to demonstrate the truth of Henri Mignet's dictum that 'if you could nail together a packing case you could build an aeroplane'. (I always used to regret that a Flying Flea never found its way to the airfield). Some stayed longer and achieved the status of hangar queens usually among members who coveted the space they were occupying. One of these was the Chrislea Ace, a refugee from Fairoaks belonging to an elderly member. I am told that the Chrislea Ace still has its devotees but having experienced a take-off from Redhill on a C of A test with only a moderate load, I offered the owner a brochure on a Robin Regent which happened to be lying around in the office and he was later persuaded to take a flight in a Regent which was in residence. His Chrislea Ace departed very shortly afterwards to be replaced by a brand new Regent!

There were many other unusual types to be spotted in the hangar at Redhill over the years but one of the most unusual and one which always intrigued me was the Alaparma Baldo registered I-DONP.

The Alaparma Baldo was a side by side two seat pusher powered by a 75 HP Praga engine. Its tailplane was supported by twin booms and braced by cables stretched to the wings. Its undercarriage consisted of two small wheels in tandem operating on bungees, outriggers on the wing tips and a skid on the nose. This highly original configuration was made even more bizarre by a fearsome sharks mouth painted on the nose! Apparently the type was originally built for the Italian air force in 1947. Anyway the arrival of

I-DONP at Redhill late in 1966 caused a minor sensation. The aircraft had flown from Italy first landing at Gatwick. Almost immediately the pilot and owner offered a flight to one of the Club's youthful hangar helpers. I heard the story later: "We took off on the southern peri track because the airfield was waterlogged, we only just made it because the bungees on one of the wheels was u/s; we made a very rapid circuit and lurched back on to the ground; one of the rudder cables had broken"! Around this time the Baldo also made one flight to Exeter, where the owner lived. Here again it caused a minor sensation particularly when the story was put about that it had flown from Italy across the Alps! But later after its return to the hangar the owner appeared to lose interest and the little pusher found a space in the far corner to acquire the reputation of a hangar queen and to gather dust.

However some considerable time later during one summer Sunday when all the aircraft had left either to a Club display elsewhere or on some jaunt across the Channel, I was on stand by in the hangar both as Duty Pilot and Club engineer. As was my custom I was profiting from the occasion to sweep the hangar floor and to remove the numerous patches of oil left by the departing Gipsy Majors. One of the members, Mike Forge, turned up to give me a hand. Mike was an Army officer in the Royal Signals who a long time later was to lose his life in the Falklands. At the time although he had a PPL, he did not have enough hours to qualify for flying membership. After we had finished our sweeping, I noticed that Mike was spending a good deal of time examining the Baldo which was sitting forlornly in the corner of the hangar covered with dust. Then he came over to me and said: "No harm in pushing her out and giving her a good wash. I've pumped up the tyres and sorted the bungees". I thought to myself that the owner who had gone off to fly for Zambia Airways would not object to that. So we pushed the Baldo into the sunshine. After he had finished cleaning the aircraft Mike said: "No harm in giving the engine a run". I thought that the owner was not likely to object to that and I had my doubts whether the engine would start. Mike then swung the prop and the engine burst into life. He yelled: "No harm in taxiing around for a bit to check the brakes and the steering "! Mike then proceeded to taxi all over the deserted airfield with the note of the engine noise rising from time to time. Then inevitably it happened. I saw that the Baldo was airborne in the circuit! After landing, Mike taxied back to the hangar and silently we pushed the machine back into its usual place. I was speechless! Mike said: "Sorry the throttle got stuck". I said: "Better not mention it"!

In 1968 the following advertisement appeared in the Exchange and Mart. 'Two seat ultra light I-DONP, 75 HP pusher, Vampire type, requires permit, seen Tiger Club, Redhill £525 ono. BOX ZAMBIA 3722. Shortly afterwards the Baldo was dismantled and removed from the hangar by road. Maybe the owner got tired of paying the hangarage bills. The people who acquired it told me that enquiries had been made to the Italian civil aviation authorities as to its airworthiness status. A reply had been received to the effect that if they had known that I-DONP was about to leave Italy, they would have done their best to prevent its departure. As for airworthiness, there was no question of issuing a certificate not even for export. A long time later I-DONP achieved a British registration and was seen at Lydd but I was told that it never acquired a Permit to Fly.

The Caithness Saga

In 1963 the Tiger Club organised an expedition to the very north of Scotland to put on an airshow. The adventure later became known as the 'Caithness Saga' and there were many stories told including this one from James Gilbert:

I borrow a Land Rover and drive through high-hedged, dewy country lanes to Castletown airfield. No-one else is about, and except for the skylarks and curlews the landscape is deserted. I untie my Turbulent, start it up, and take off to John O'Groats, the northernmost point of the mainland of Britain. I turn out to sea towards the misty shapes of the Orkney Islands. Orkney itself bigger than the others is wreathed in Harr, covered by a thick curving mist generated as that moist sea air flows over its shores.

It was my ambition to land there, so remote and strange are these islands. I turn back to Stroma, a little island clear of fog, shining in the sunshine. At one end is a lighthouse, huge and white; I circle it at low altitude, then drop down over the sea for a low run alongside its beacon tower. Beside it is a monstrous foghorn like a giant's saxophone, and I aim my tiny Turbulent right at it, as if I intended flying down its vast black throat. Just as I pull up over the top, some wit who has been watching me sounds it off, in a monstrous cow-like Moo, deafening even above the noise of my engine, a roar that almost frightens me out of my seat and into the sea.

If I cannot land on Orkney, perhaps I can on Stroma. True it has no aerodrome, or indeed anything else much, and true it would be an illegal and foolhardy thing to do, but there is one field of sheep-cropped island turf that looks smooth and level and just about long enough. I have always made it a rule never to land in any strange field that I have not walked over first to inspect but is not to-day a good day for breaking rules? I drag the field twice from a low altitude, then set up my approach.

Low and fairly slow, it looks plenty long, so need to slow right up for a really short landing. Touch down in a perfect three-pointer, and run on, slightly uphill, towards the end of the field. Run on and on, unaccountably she will not slow down, uphill though it is. Brakes on a Turbulent are differential only, for steering while taxiing, but you can obtain some braking action from them by pumping the rudder pedals from side to side. I pump with increasing terror as the end of the field looms up ahead. With fifty yards to go it is bitter certain knowledge that I am not going to stop before reaching that solid stake and wire sheep fence. At the last minute I turn the careening beast sharp right towards rough ground and a ditch; she leaps and bounds, the tail comes up, and the whole aeroplane dives with a deafening crash nose-first into the ditch. There is a rending splintering sound as the propeller disintegrates, then absolute stark silence, I am hanging face down in my straps in the wreck of my aeroplane as it sits, tail in the air, nose in the ground. I undo my straps and clamber down over the wing. I am near to tears, on the edge of the ditch.

I am an idiot. A three-hundred hour idiot. I will be drummed out of the Tiger Club. My friends will never speak to me again. It will take a month to get the wreck off this lonely island back again to be rebuilt. I will be prosecuted for every flying offence in the book. I will be penniless for years trying to pay for fines and repairs. I have done something so stupid that I can hardly believe it. There cannot be more than one boat a week to this forsaken islet; I will not even be able to leave the scene of my crime for days.

The curlews call and the waves lap against the nearby rocks. Somewhere a sheep is baaing; "baa", it says, "idiot, idiot baa". Mechanically I take hold of the tail of the Turbulent and pull her out of the shallow ditch. Strange, there doesn't seem to be much wrong with the airframe. But the propeller must be smashed to a million pieces. But there is only four inches snapped cleanly off one end of the tiny blade. Still what use is any prop with four inches missing off one blade, unless of course… and a mad idea begins to form in my mind. To-day I must have gone really crazy. Suppose you sawed off four inches of the other blade, and could get it to balance?

Normally these VW engines turn at about 3000 rpm in this installation. But I own a VW car and I know the engine in that. It turns at 4000 rpm for long periods, cruising flat out with no damage. At 4000 rpm I would be getting more horses out of the engine, perhaps enough to offset the inefficiency of the cut down propeller. Enough to take off from here? For the first time since my recent abrupt arrival I take a good look at where I am. For a start I was trying to land with a 5 knot tailwind. And this field has a deceptive double curvature so that the lip over which I touched down was not the lip at the end of the field but a false one half way down! I was trying to land downwind, using only half the available space!

Over the dewy turf on a tractor comes one of the island's inhabitants and addresses me in a Pictish, Gaelic, Orkney accent that is next to impossible to comprehend. Could he I ask him find me a hacksaw somewhere on the island? He thinks the lighthouse people have one and drives off to ask. There is a little village of crofts in the centre of the island. It is a mediaeval village; there are no roads or gardens, each croft being surrounded by a rolling sea of green turf, criss-crossed by tracks where the inhabitants of Stroma have been in the habit of walking to work, or to each other's houses.

Till he returns I burn with impatience. The hacksaw comes and with it I bite off the other tip. What is left is a sad runt of a propeller, but I start up the engine and it runs smoothly and sweetly. I swear that there is less vibration than ever before. Full power revs are not excessive, and taxiing up and down the field seems to reveal no lack of acceleration. I strap up and back up to the topmost corner of the field. I taxi at full throttle down the field. Yes, I think she would have flown there. Once more then the real attempt. At first it seems doomed to failure, not to say disaster, then the tail lifts and we slowly gather speed, at the far end of the field, yellow with fright, half stalled, we get airborne. Soon we are properly flying, at a decent speed and altitude, very chastened back towards the mainland….

A Tiger's Tale or a Check Pilot's Nightmare.

Check flying and in particular the initial Tiger Moth check which every new member had to take occasionally caused problems. In this story 'GB' referred to Arthur Golding-Barrett, a very well-known character in the Club who was the Club's Senior Check Pilot at the time. Barry Griffiths wrote this story.

I arrived at the Club some time ago looking forward to a good day's flying. It was cold and clear and the sun was shining brightly. "Ha", said GB. "Morning, just the fella I'm looking for. Got a chap down to-day for a check, nice fella, you'll like him. Just like you to ride round with him, see if he knows. Bound to be all right".

I was introduced to the Smooth Young Man who was obviously very sure of himself. GB went off muttering about duty pilots and landing tees and I was left with the SYM. He told me that he had done lots and lots of hours; to be specific nearly 103 hours - all solo of course. I checked his PPL number (God, there can't be that many pilots in this country!), and we discussed the procedure of the check. "It will be on a Tiger of course," I said. His composure slipped a little. "Oh, well I've flown a Tiger naturally. I mean, I've handled most Club planes, you know. But it has been a rather long time”. Perhaps he would like to postpone the flight and get some Tiger dual? “Oh, good gracious no, I can manage perfectly well”.

Outside the hangar CDC sat quiet and dignified between the Cub and the stocky Stampe. SYM made straight for the latter and began to install himself. By the time I got to him he was strapped in. He didn’t even blush. “I must say, it looks very much like a Tiger”, he said, as he clambered aboard CDC. Against pre-flight inspection I wrote ′Not carried out’. Although the sun still shone, it seemed to have got suddenly colder. “I can’t seem to find the switches”, said SYM. “They’re outside on the b…. fuselage”, said John, whose fingers were obviously getting cold. He nearly had them warmed too quickly a moment later when SYM switched on the mags. “Sorry, old boy, thought you said switches on”. We got to the take-off point with only two marker boards to our credit, and SYM began his checks. This seemed to revolve round ‘pitch, gyros, carb heat and brakes’ and it took a determined attempt before I could get him to unlock the slats. It seemed that Ercoupes and Colts were not equipped with a similar device. Before I could fully grasp the implications of that last remark the take-off was in progress. For the first yard or so the stick was held fully back. Then SYM remembered what his undercarriage looked like and pushed the stick fully forward CDC swung smoothly off the runway assisted by a slight crosswind, and set course for the pump house with the tail getting progressively higher. Realising his mistake, SYM reversed the process and pulled the stick fully back. CDC leapt into the air, stalled, and returned to earth, fortunately upon three points, with a bone jarring shock. This must have upset SYM’s confidence because at this point he released the controls. CDC, bristling with wounded dignity, bounced back into the air and with open slats bore down upon the hangar. It was about this time that I discovered that there was no stick in the front cockpit! A quick look in the mirror revealed SYM's white face with his eyes shut tight. But CDC was not to retire so easily. At full throttle she flashed over the hangar roof. I had a fleeting glimpse of a certain very senior member covered with mud and shaking his fists and we were climbing safely away. SYM's return to the controls was obvious when the aircraft began to skid and wallow. It occurred to me that if I were to acquaint him with the situation he might panic and do something silly, so I decided to continue with the check as though all were well. We managed medium and steep turns without losing more than 2000 feet and we then climbed to 8000 feet for the stalling check. I had some difficulty in making myself heard, but eventually SYM realised that I wanted him to lock the slats. "Right-ho", he said, and without further ado pulled the trimmer fully back! CDC promptly stood upon her tail and hung vertically, in complete silence. Then without warning the nose dropped in a vicious hammerhead and the old aeroplane flicked into a spin. "0oooh!" said a voice from somewhere behind me. Eventually brute force triumphed – a foot behind the elevator trimmer did the trick, and as the trimmer went fully forward, SYM relinquished the controls for a second time. The spin stopped immediately but the nose kept going down. CDC had obviously had enough. Negative 'G' wrenched my clipboard free, and I automatically grabbed it, releasing the trimmer in the process. By this time we were well beyond the vertical and the negative 'G' was still building up, so that I couldn't get my arms down into the cockpit. Speed was increasing rapidly and soon the inevitable happened. The slipstream wrenched the clipboard out of my hands. It hurtled backwards and caught SYM a resounding blow on the head. His face was bright red due to the negative ‘G’ and my eyes felt as though they were swelling. At last the ‘G’ started to reduce as CDC approached the vertical again in an inverted climb. As soon as I could get my arms down I pulled the trimmer fully back. This as I later realised was a mistake. CDC fell on her back and again the nose dropped. After so much negative ‘G’ application of positive ‘G’ caused both SYM and me to grey out. The old Tiger roared down into the bottom of a loop, and as the nose started to rise, I dimly saw something flash over my head below the fuel tank and simultaneously I heard another screech from SYM. It was the clipboard again second time round. As CDC arrived at the top of the loop she stalled and flicked the right way up. Having demonstrated her displeasure she settled into a steady glide.

SYM was for the time being uninterested, the second blow from the clipboard had been a heavy one. I opened the throttle gently and trimmed forward. CDC purred on her way smoothly and contentedly towards Redhill. Having disposed of stalling, spinning and aerobatics in one fell swoop, I felt that I might be entitled to postpone the remainder of the check. Hollow moans from the direction of the empennage suggested that SYM had returned to the land of the living. After some persuasion backed by suitable adjectives, SYM took control for a normal circuit and landing.

In the light of what followed I was very pleased that I hadn’t asked for something less conventional. SYM’s approach surprised me considerably; it was normal! That is until we reached the height to check. At this point SYM slowly eased the stick forward! We hit the ground with a bang that would have destroyed a lesser aeroplane. Needless to say we bounced! At a rough guess I would say 60 feet. In self preservation I opened the throttle wide. With her slats gasping for air CDC sank towards the ground. I was beginning to think that we would make it when SYM again pushed the stick forward. Indestructible the Tiger hit and bounced. I closed the throttle just before the impact but she still bounced about 50 feet.

At long last we ran out of airfield and speed, and completed a neat ground loop. As SYM taxied back to the hangar, I was wondering whether to resign immediately or to flee the country. We arrived outside the hangar to be confronted with a row of solemn faces. "Switch off and open the throttle", I told SYM. Out of the corner of my eye I saw the fuel cock move to the 'Off' position. And before I could stop him he opened the throttle! CDC charged the assembled onlookers who very wisely scattered in all directions. We became airborne just as we entered the hangar which fortunately was empty. SYM realised his mistake immediately; he kept full power on and made a very tight 180 turn inside the hangar. It was the tightest turn I had ever seen. CDC shot out of the hangar again, when the engine having run out of fuel coughed and died. SYM instinctively pulled the stick back to maintain height and CDC stalled and dropped onto the grass in a perfect three pointer: Of course after a display of airmanship like that I was bound to pass him and to-day he is one of the Club's foremost pilots.

Beware of GB when he walks up to you and says "You're just the fella I'm looking for!"

Golf Courses

Golf and light aircraft do not often go together but sometimes they do. Michael Jones has this story:

Philip Falk was an elderly Tiger Club member who seemed to have two passions in life – flying and golf. Small, round faced, bespectacled and always with a cheery grin, he used to book an aircraft at Redhill without fail and almost religiously every Saturday morning. Also nearly always this was for a flight either to Headcorn or Fairoaks in one of the Club's cabin types since following a minor taxiing accident in CDC, he had decided, it was said, to leave the biplanes to the younger generation. Besides Philip would have been the first to admit that he was not one of the Club's best performers on a Tiger Moth. However he did not lack flying experience. On one occasion when a Spitfire had been parked in the hangar overnight and a crowd was standing round it in awe and admiration, Philip strolled cheerfully past, muttering: "Nice old things, Spitfires. I really used to enjoy flying them"!

As for golf Philip used to play at Betchworth Park, a course the other side of Reigate where he was a member. Since I had recently taken up the game and was mildly hooked, occasionally I used to play a round with him there during which time we used to have endless discussions on the suitability of this fairway or that for landing the Super Cub. Needless to say at the airfield people did not talk very much about golf but very occasionally the Club's Jodel Musketeer could be observed outside the hangar being loaded up with four golf bags in its huge rear locker and four people preparing for a flight in eager anticipation of a round of golf at Le Touquet. Philip used to pester me repeatedly to organise a similar trip but I was never persuaded. In my opinion golf and flying did not fit easily together.

However one day Philip rang me in great excitement to say that the Secretary of the Betchworth Park Golf Club had given him permission to land on the course in the Super Cub and that he would be delighted to meet the Secretary of the Tiger Club at the same time. In the interest of good relations between fliers and golfers it was an invitation I could not refuse. So the flight took place one summer's afternoon and the landing was made on the one suitable fairway. Philip having been in the public relations business knew how to organise a reception committee and consequently I was made very welcome. An unremarkable event one might say in the daily life of a flying club but one that gave me a good deal of pleasure and satisfaction.

However my previous experience of landing on a golf course was not quite so happy. Way back in the 1960s when Fairoaks was an uncontrolled grass aerodrome, the Tiger Club used to recruit quite a few members who flew there; in fact so much so that there was a branch established on the airfield and quite often I used to ferry various Club aircraft to be hangared there for the benefit of local members. The Fairoaks Aero Club operated Condors and Piper Colts on lease for ab initio training. The Piper Colt was a very useful aircraft to obtain a PPL in the shortest possible time and also in the winter months at Fairoaks with its large nose wheel it coped remarkably well with the notoriously boggy ground.

One particular mid winter afternoon I had ferried a Jodel Ambassadeur to Fairoaks and for one reason or another I had not arranged a pick-up for the return flight to Redhill. Consequently I was offered a flight back in a Piper Colt to be flown by one of the assistant instructors. There were snow showers developing in the area but we did not think that we would have any difficulty in avoiding them. However very soon after taking off we ran into an enormous snow storm from which we could find no escape. Having attempted to turn back we were soon hopelessly lost in the swirling snow flakes; the ground was very quickly disappearing and the horizon had long since vanished. I came to the rapid conclusion that in such conditions I would have preferred to be in almost any aircraft other than a Piper Colt with basic instruments! But suddenly as we blundered lower and lower, I spotted what appeared to be a golf course immediately beneath us. I yelled to my companion: "Let's get down there!". He needed no further persuasion; he closed the throttle and we, so to speak, almost immediately arrived on a short stretch of fairway miraculously avoiding some bunkers. Mercifully there was no-one on the course which was hardly surprising given the blizzard conditions. After a very short distance we rumbled up a small incline and finished up on a green circling the pin at a slow walking pace. As we got out of the aircraft and started to look for the Club house my opinion of the Piper Colt went up a notch or two! Eventually we stumbled on the building and explained to a horrified Club Secretary what had happened. It turned out to be a highly exclusive golf club well inside the London Control Zone. We were allowed one phone call back to Fairoaks and then were ushered out of the premises without further delay. The Secretary required no reports and no investigations. The last thing he wished to see was a picture in the local newspaper of a Piper Colt perched on one of his hallowed greens. The Colt was flown out next morning without incident and without publicity and that was the end of the affair.

I still play golf quite regularly on various courses which are usually picturesque, with escarpments, lakes, trees and slopes in all directions. I still muse on which fairway I would prefer to land if I had to. I fear that golf fairways will never make ideal landing strips but it would be nice if small grass aerodromes would look a bit more like golf courses but flat, needless to say, and without bunkers and greens!

Messing about in Boats

No collection of Tales from the Tiger Rag would be complete without one on the seaplane by Jonny Seccombe.

Was it Rattie or was it toad who said something to the effect that there is nothing absolutely nothing like messing about in boats? Of course neither of them had wings, nor did Grahame say anything about aeroplanes or even Tiger Moths in his stories, but for those whose attention is divided between boats and aeroplanes, where does Mike go on those weekends away from Redhill? I might find it interesting to combine the two. I have always had a desire to fly up the fjords of Norway in a floatplane or amphibian, so as the first step in that venture I found it irresistible this summer to drive down to Rye for long week-ends to learn to fly a floatplane.

Anyone who suggests that a Tiger Moth has sluggish controls, a slow roll rate, a stiff rudder and less than sparkling performance, plus a continuous need to be looked after and administered to has obviously never flown a sea Tiger. It is a terrible aeroplane in the air; ailerons are totally ineffective, you need both feet on the rudder bar to shift it either way and all the speeds are the same, 65 knots. But on the water it is fun, real fun!

My first day at Scotney Court it was blowing a stiff 25 knots, enough to ground all but the most intrepid flyers at Redhill. The seaplane was in its element. 'Swing' turns could only be performed by the most skilful while the 'hump' turns when you reverse the normal weather-cocking characteristics, were the order of the day. Long periods of taxiing, porpoising and skipping were interspersed with short circuits for a little relaxation, eventually culminating in that extra little rating on the licence.

And so plans for Scotland were made. The car had to be serviced and new road maps purchased. Somebody was bound to have a 'half mil' you could borrow but woe betides if the arrival party lost its way. Memories of batting over the plain behind Blackpool at 500 feet to reduce the headwind and skimming over the waves across Morecambe bay at 50 feet will always be with me. Tom Freer taking control and diving across the hills into a cloud shrouded Windermere was a moment that could never be experienced in a landplane. As long as you can see the water you are going to be OK in a seaplane. Whoever tired of flying round a cloud infested lake at low altitude?

Have you ever spent two weeks on a flying holiday camping beside the tailplane and covering hundreds of miles without seeing an airfield or another aircraft apart from low flying jet trainers? Have you ever wanted to see the Lake District or the Scottish lochs from close quarters without infringing the 500 foot rule or wondering about the ditching characteristics of your aeroplane? Have you ever thought what it would be like to sweep past a 1930s lake steamer on the step of a 1940s Tiger? Have you ever turned on to finals knowing there was absolutely no need to look up long finals to check there was no cross-country circuit merchant about to slice into your wing tip?

IVW may be slow on floats; she may be more in her element on wheels during the winter but as Toad said (or was it Rattie): “There’s nothing like messing about in boats”.

The Toothpick

The pylon racing movement otherwise known as Formula I played a very large part in the life of the Tiger Club during the 1970s. Michael Jones who was the secretary and later chairman of the British Formula Air Racing Association has not forgotten this incident:

I cannot remember who first called it the 'toothpick' but the name was certainly appropriate for this particular propeller; only 56 inches in diameter and very fine in pitch with sharply pointed tips, its trailing edge practically cut your hand when swinging it to start the engine of a Rollason Beta. It was of course a metal racing prop for use on midget racers. At the time, 1970, the Tiger Club had two Betas on strength, 'Forerunner' and 'Blue Chip'. They had been constructed in a converted squash court at Redhill aerodrome, and assembled and finished off in the Club hangar by Jim Ellis and John Sarratt.

The first Formula 1 air race to take place outside the USA had been held earlier that year in the Isle of Man, three Betas and two slab wing Cassutts had taken part. The Cassutts had been built by Tom Storey using kits imported from America and they also had been assembled and finished in the hangar at Redhill. In that historic first race in the Isle of Man the Beta 'Forerunner' had just pipped the Cassutt 'Firestreak' by a few feet in a very exciting finish. Needless to say following this event there was a good deal of friendly rivalry at Redhill both in the air and on the ground.

It is best to draw a veil over the origins of the 'toothpick' and how it was acquired by the Tiger Club. Like most F/1 racing props it had probably been manufactured by Sensenich and subsequently unofficially modified. But its history was unknown and frankly in the heady atmosphere of the time no-one was particularly interested. All that mattered was: would it make a Beta go faster than a Cassutt? It had proved itself on 'Forerunner' in the Isle of Man, but in later events that season 'Firestreak' had established a superiority and now I was determined to try it out on the second Beta 'Blue Chip' which had just been modified with Cassutt type 'go faster' cowlings and a prop extension, the idea being, of course, to win the last two races of the season scheduled at Shobdon and Teesside.

In the search for full throttle speed, testing a propeller or any other modification for that matter was not a haphazard exercise. For some time already at Redhill a test course of sorts had been established between the line of the hangars and the tower on top of Leith Hill, a distance there and back of approximately 20 miles. In relation to the measured distance and the time taken a table of speeds in mph to three decimal places had been calculated and carefully drawn up. The starts and finishes were both timed and observed at Redhill. On this occasion on that early evening in September 1970 I was being observed and timed by Frank Gathercole and Steve Thompson. Frank was a garage owner from south London who had been hooked on F/1 racing and had bought the second of Tom Storey's Cassutts which he called 'Hopalong', Steve was very well known at the Club and much later was to make a name for himself by coming second in the Formula 1 championships at Reno in his own long winged Cassutt.

About a minute into the timed flight somewhere in the vicinity of Betchworth, there was suddenly an appallingly loud bang followed by a severe grinding vibration. Sensing that some catastrophe had occurred to the engine, I instinctively closed the throttle, whereupon the engine stopped completely with the propeller stationary in the vertical position. My first reaction was one of relief that the frightening vibration had ceased and that all was now peace and quiet in an aircraft which was in fact quite a good glider. However gliding around over the Surrey countryside in an engineless Beta was not an experience to be enjoyed for ever. They say that the prospect of a forced landing concentrates the mind wonderfully and I was now determined to get the little beast on the ground without damage and to avoid all the pain and grief that would ensue if I made a mess of it.

Luckily there was a field of sorts available; perhaps I had half noticed it on previous test runs. However a sideslip and a conventional three point landing a third of the way into the field was not an option on a Beta. The aircraft did not sideslip well and without flaps or airbrakes it had distressing habit of floating interminably in the tree point attitude; the only thing for it was to get the wheels on the ground as close to the near hedge as possible and rely on the brakes to kill the speed. Mercifully this technique worked although I could have sworn that the wheel spats touched something on the way in and as 'Blue Chip' shuddered to a halt a few feet from the far hedge I offered a silent prayer of thanks to the toe operated Goodyear disc brakes fitted in recognition of the fact that it was Goodyear who had sponsored the first Formula 1 meetings in America more than twenty years earlier.

Trembling I got out of the cockpit to notice with stupefaction that three quarters of one blade of the 'toothpick' was missing, the blade, so to speak, that was out of sight in the air. I also noticed that there was something odd about the cowlings but it was now time to get to a phone and summon help from the hangar at Redhill and "bring the trailer and the tools", I shouted as I put the phone down. (Fortunately Betas were designed to be easily dismantled and purpose built trailers were available.)

Steve and Frank duly arrived and while dismantling the wings, it was decided to remove what was left of the 'toothpick' and the engine. As we detached the many screws holding the cowlings in place, we found that it was necessary to support the engine by hand to prevent it falling to the ground and I saw with horror that three of the four arms of the engine bearers had snapped like carrots and the fourth was badly kinked. The engine had been held in place during the forced landing by the cowlings and it was then that I offered a second silent prayer of thanks to Jim Ellis who had installed the new cowlings so meticulously and so securely. Never again would I complain that it used to take half an hour to remove them! The Beta was soon repaired in time to take part in the last race meeting of the season at Teesside, an event completely ruined by fog.

The following year, 1971, after a successful first F/1 meeting of the season at North Weald there was a fatal accident to an Owl racer whilst it was being ferried back to Redhill. The propeller this time a modified Macauley had failed and the engine had become separated from the airframe in flight. Very soon after this it was decided with the support of the Air Registration Board to set up the

Formula Air Racing Association with a strong technical sub-committee to supervise and control amongst everything else the use and maintenance of metal racing propellers. Although the Sensenich metal racing prop continued to be used by practically everyone, they had to be brand new, only used on the race course itself within specific RPM bands, equipped with their own log books and subject to a regime of regular inspections and crack tests. John Sarratt found himself very busy in his spare time manufacturing special boxes for their safe storage and transport to race meetings. Some time later on the principle of precaution all F/1 racers both in Britain and the USA were required to fit cables to their engines to secure them to the airframe in the event of catastrophic propeller failure.

As for the missing blade of the 'toothpick' it never turned up and as for the Leith Hill test run it fell into disuse.

Displays Abroad

Tiger Club aircraft frequently participated in flying events organised on the other side of the channel and sometimes members provided their own machines which were displayed under the Club banner. In 1975 the Vice-Chairman acquired the Arrow Active from the Club and loaned it for a display in Denmark. Brian Smith told the story:

Since the Arrow Active was built in 1932 it has not as far as it is known ventured across the Channel and after reading this tale people will probably understand why! A request had been received from some Danish friends at short notice for a display at a big rally being organised in 1977 at Herning, a large town half way up Jutland. I volunteered to take the Active and Neil Williams joined me in his own Bucker Jungmann.

We met up at Shoreham on one glorious Friday morning to clear Customs; they really are the most friendly bunch down there and we set off into a 15 knot headwind bound for Seppe in Holland which was a little over two hours away. Neil's Jungmann was the critical aeroplane with 2½ hours available compared with 4 hours for the Active but both seemed to manage a 95 to 100 knot cruise comfortably. Anyway we eventually arrived over Seppe and there the fun and games started with a 12 knot cross wind blowing across the only runway which at least was grass. The Active's landing characteristics are well known and suffice to say cross wind landings are not on; with no alternative down we went and after much pedalling and gunning of the engine the Active found itself intact on foreign soil for the first time in 45 years.

After a nervous cup of coffee and a spot of lunch we set off for Wilhemshaven. Again it was a pleasant flight albeit into that blasted head wind but we arrived just over two hours later to find the same cross wind situation but this time on a tarmac runway. By this time it began to dawn on me why nobody had ever tried to go abroad in the Active. I gingerly touched down on the main wheels keeping the tail up until it would stay up no longer; so far so good but then there was a hint of drift to the left and trying to correct it to the right there was no response from the back end. Blast! It's going to go.... Quick! Pick a gap in the runway lights, point through the gap and hope for the best. At a terrifying speed (which on reflection was about 10 knots) the aircraft and I left the runway with neither of us in control until we came to a halt several seconds later. Retrieving my heart from my boots I stepped out of the machine and proceeded to taxi whilst walking beside it, a technique I had seen demonstrated by certain senior members of the Club in the past.

We were away an hour later bound for Herning. Although flying east, we were also heading north, so we figured that dusk would fall around 20.00 hours local time. This would have been about right if it were not for a mass of cloud which appeared on the western horizon and prematurely cut off the daylight like somebody turning off a switch. By 7.30 I couldn't read a map, at 7.35 I couldn't see the compass and by 7.40 I was formating on the flames of the Jungmann's stub exhausts. The town of Herning was lit up five minutes away and we had marked the airfield as being three miles north of it but what it consisted of was anybody's guess. We arrived over the town and duly flew north for two minutes; I then made the mistake of glancing at my watch only to look up and see the Jungmann in the final stage of a wing rock, turn on its side and slip down into the gloom. I followed as quick as I could but my worst fear was confirmed when Neil disappeared and there was no way that I could find him. It is difficult to describe the feelings that came over me at that moment: fear, panic, and apathy to name but a few. However with the brain re-activated, I came to the conclusion that Neil must have seen something and the chances were that he had found the airfield.

Meanwhile down on 'terra firma' a different form of panic was taking place. The locals were expecting us but with the onset of darkness they had convinced themselves that we had diverted somewhere else. There they were sitting in their clubhouse knocking back beer and sandwiches when the drone of two unsynchronised aero engines came to their ears. It must have been like an air raid warning with people throwing themselves out of every available exit to see what was going on. By the time they realised that it was the long lost British contingent, pandemonium had set in with people leaping into anything with wheels and racing to construct the most bizarre flare path imaginable with car headlights pointing up the approach. Neil landed in the middle of the lot and ended up in a sand pit. He jumped out of his Jungmann and told everybody in no uncertain terms to turn their cars round before they blinded me as well. While all of this was going on, I was flying round in ever decreasing circles convincing myself that the best thing to do was to spin in and get it over and done with! But suddenly I spied a large flock of sheep which on closer inspection turned out to be fifty or more spamcans parked together and there was the runway together with an invisible audience. The jubilation turned to gloom when I realised that yet again I was faced with a cross wind landing on tarmac but this time at night. Anyway down I went and found the ground, trying again to keep the tail up as long as possible. Down it came eventually and with the sheet of flame coming out of the engine and the trail of sparks from the tail skid on the runway, there must have been a veritable firework display. Luckily we stayed on the runway and soon crowds of Danes flocked round us to discover how we had managed to find the airfield without VOR or some other gimmick.

The rest of the trip was a bit of an anti-climax after that. We flew the display the next day in torrential rain and a 400 foot cloud base which was a novel experience looping off the deck and finding oneself in cloud going over the top. On our return the wind went round180 degrees and the rain continued until we crossed the Dutch border on Sunday afternoon. During our trip we accumulated more than 14 hours of flying and looking back I suppose it was fun but was I glad to push the Active back into the hangar at Redhill on Sunday evening !

Reno 'The Empire Strikes Back'

Formula 1 pylon racing in the early 1980s was being dominated in the UK and France by Steve Thompson who had designed and built a new wing for his Cassutt. Since 1970 when F/1 racing had started in Britain, average speeds had increased dramatically round the three mile course. In 1983, assisted by Tom Storey as his crew chief, Steve decided to take on the Americans at their own game at Reno, the Mecca for all pylon racing. He finished second in the final 'Gold' race at the remarkable speed of 225 mph. So the Americans gave his machine the name above. Here is Steve's account of the event:

Around June '83 we British racers learnt that two of the French contingent were planning to take their racers to Reno. This made me think of ways of doing the same because it would have been very poor if the French had beaten us to it. I found out that there was a chartered Tristar flight to Los Angeles and contacted the charterer to obtain his permission to take my Cassutt on his flight.

On September 6th Harvey Tring and I loaded the racer and towed it on Derek Wright's trailer to the airport. Customs proved to be no problem and Bangor, Maine was our first stop in the USA. There the Port Director of the Customs service was most helpful and cleared the machine in as baggage. The flight continued to LA where I was delighted to find a FARA member, Bill Rogers, with a 'Renta-truck' to move the racer to Torrance airport some ten miles to the south.

I spent the next three days fitting the aircraft into a borrowed trailer for the 300 mile drive to Reno. John Parker, a former F/1 champion at Reno, generously loaned me both the trailer and the use of his hangar for any work I needed to do. After taking time off to visit the Spruce Goose in its dome at Long Beach near the Queen Mary, well worth a visit, on Saturday 10th we drove up to Reno, towing the trailer with Carol Rogers' camper van. It was an impressive drive including one hill that took five gallons of fuel to climb. We took eleven hours and averaged around 8 mpg, pretty good considering the terrain which took the road to over 6000 feet at times.

On arriving at Stead Airport I felt rather depressed as the hangar seemed to be full of very sleek looking racers. Then we retired to town for beer and burgers. On Sunday morning we rose bright and early to get the aircraft assembled. More work than normal needed to be done because I had disconnected all the plug leads and dismantled the fuel system while preparing the aircraft for its trans-Atlantic crossing. Also at this stage the engine and aircraft were cleared by the scrutineers including valve lift and clearance and swept cylinder volumes. Carburettors were also visually checked. Still we managed to get ready in time for a test flight on Sunday evening.

Monday was the first of three days for practice and qualifications, so I practised in the morning on the wood prop, recording an unofficial speed of 210 mph. I then changed to a metal prop and a different air intake. All seemed to be well so I decided to qualify that afternoon recording

226.961 mph. Qualifying continued until Wednesday night so we amused ourselves with countless minor adjustments and improvements. At the end of qualifying my aircraft was 7th fastest out of 24, putting me into heat 1C to be held on the Friday.

The objective in heat 1C was to remain in the fastest eight of all the speeds recorded in the three groups in heat 1, keeping a place in the Gold final on Sunday. The start at Reno is arranged as a line of eight aircraft abreast, three on the runway and five on the ramp. This I found rather alarming because I was one of those on the ramp and no white lines had been painted on it. Actually it was no problem, the differences in the acceleration of the aircraft provided the separation needed. Following the start lap I found myself in 4th place which I maintained to the end, just beating last year's winner John Sharp. The British camp which now included both Tom Storey and Robin Voice was well pleased with this and we retired to the cocktail party in very good spirits. On the social front we found the organisers and all the other crews very hospitable and we were provided with free rooms and the loan of a car for the week.

Saturday, the third of the public days brought more racing but no flying for me as the final was scheduled for Sunday morning. We concentrated on the great British art of psyching up the opposition and threatening international protests but put in a little more time on the racer by removing what little weight was possible, taking out all unnecessary plumbing and instruments.

The final started towards the east and I was placed on the runway, one of the three faster aircraft having a selected to take the ramp due to its smoother surface. After the 180 left turn to get back on to the course behind Wentworth,

Cote and John Dowd on a slab wing Cassutt, flying high downwind I seemed to gain rapidly on Cote and lost sight of him after a lap or so; Charles Wentworth motored off into the distance as before, leaving Dusty Dowd about 50 yards in front and below me. Finally I just managed to creep by him and dive down to finish second.

On Sunday afternoon we furiously dismantled the aircraft and drove back to LA on Monday: By Thursday evening I was home again and a terrific holiday was over.

Confessions

Maxi Gainza was an émigré from Argentina who had settled in London with his family. He was a regular contributor to Pilot magazine and later became a very keen aircraft owner.

It was a grotty January afternoon at Redhill when even Smithy stayed on the ground. Not that I was any keener than our boy ace to fly under a thousand foot overcast of strato-cus, but unlike him I had a visitor to impress – my brother-in-law from Argentina who as usual was full of horror stories about flying in the Pampas which he, a low houred private pilot like myself acquitted himself far too well for my ego. I had no choice but to strap him into old TKC and take off into the drizzle blowing in from the west.

But not for just a few bumps round the circuit. I had a far better idea. Well, glider pilots could do it – or was it pigeons? So could I in fact. I knew I could take a Stampe through cloud, thanks to a memorable escapade with Brendan the day his seat belt came undone halfway through a slow roll. But that is another story and, needless to say, Wonder Boy is still with us, thank God, and very much reformed too!

In any event once airborne I set course on a steady climb due east, and putting on my clipped English accent for period effect I informed my Argentine compatriot up front that we were going on top, no need to flap, old chap, piece of cake, really….

And so it was. A few tense minutes later, eyes glued to the compass and the turn-and-bank indicator, the enveloping milkiness grew brighter; there was a flash of blue above me and suddenly we were punching through rose-tinted cloud tops and slowly rising over a vast empty sea of bundled mohair into clear sky. Twisting my head round I saw the twin trail of inward-curling spirals whipped up by our wings as we climbed out of those vapoury depths.

I poled the Stampe round 180 degrees and slow rolled it into the setting sun, then half rolled again and let it drop inverted, stomach butterflies a-flutter, until we were skimming over the cloud tops and occasionally ripping through them in heart-stopping flashes of golden light. We turned back due east mindful of holding our position relative to the ground, and tail-chased our shadow over tumbling valleys and twisting ravines and billowing slopes, all the while yahooing into our masks and thinking "this is the life."

Sunset was soon upon us though, and it was with great reluctance and hardly any sense of urgency that I turned my mind to the task of getting us back to Redhill, I reckoned couldn't be more than five minutes away. So I should be down before the sun sank in the horizon. What I didn't know was that by then it would be well past sunset on the ground, that indeed it was already getting dark under that pastel-coloured blanket of cloud.

I let down on a northerly heading and again after some tense minutes watching the altimeter wind down to 800 feet, Marcelo called out that he could see a wide river beneath us! Yes, so could I, all through streaming rain, plus no end of shipping and floodlit decks and red-eyed chimney stacks and aerials, and far off on our port beam, the odd million lights turning on in deepening gloom, beckoning Londoners home to tea.

In a flash I had reversed course and reached out for the nav. chart, but it was already too dark to map read. Now you may say that any self-respecting Tiger Club member can find Redhill from anywhere within a 50-mile radius – specially aboard TKC. But I was still a newcomer to these shores, and as for Marcelo, all he could offer was moral support which he did rattling away inanely about how magic and dé jà vu it all was, the wind in the wires, rainy London sliding beneath us, sweet Thames running softly, and how about picking a field before night closed in on us?

They all seemed uncomfortably small and square except for one longish strip of grass at the edge of a wood and cut at both ends by more trees. I circled low over the field once – not that I could make out much detail in that failing light – and slip-spiralled in to land.

It was only a precautionary landing but in my book it rated as a full emergency. Hence my priorities: first and foremost to survive. Second (having skimmed the trees and secured the field), walk out of it. Third (an overgrown ditch suddenly materialising in the middle of the field in line with my approach and the plane now sinking fast), remember Michael!

I gunned the throttle to counteract the sink and ruddered from danger and landed no worse than I would have done at Redhill behind the spinney (alas now gone) which screened the touchdown area for 26 from uncharitable eyes outside the Club hangar. We stopped with room to spare all in one piece to be greeted by the relentless applause of cold rain on the plane's fabric and on our leather helmets. It hardly seemed to matter.

There was a footpath leading through the woods towards some lights I had seen during the approach. By the time we reached the first door of a row of houses and rang the bell we were thoroughly drenched and looking perhaps a trifle alarming in our bulky clothes and glistening helmets. But not for Mrs. Norrie.

"Oh, you must be the pilots"! a small woman in her late forties with permed dark hair and twinkling eyes cried out flinging the door open. "Come in, you poor boys, my you are wet!", and she showed us into a tiny sitting room before we could utter words to the effect that we had come in peace. Then she briskly introduced us to her mother, an old smiling lady propped up on a sofa at the back of the room. Then she said:

"We heard you circling overhead and I knew you were looking for a place to land. Then we stopped hearing you and I thought – there they've found it! You picked the right field – the only good one in the area." How could she know I wondered stepping out of my sodden flying suit and letting her bundle away our gear. "A young RAF pilot force-landed his Hurricane on that field back in 1940 during the Battle of Britain", she went on laying the suits out by the electric fire. "It all happened right above our heads, you know…. He rang our doorbell just like you. He asked if he could use the telephone – as I am sure you will. Here give them a call while I get you some tea."

She disappeared into the kitchen leaving me to the delicate task of ringing the Club to inform them that the Stampe was slowly filling up with rainwater in a field near Tonbridge.

"Is the plane alright?" "Yes, Michael – so are we by the

way." "Are there any cows in the field?" "Not that I could see." (Cows have a weakness for doped fabric I am told). "Well, make sure that there aren't any and that you tie the plane down for the night. See you in the morning."

Only now could I enjoy my tea and being mothered by Mrs Norrie. She called a friend to drive us into town and back to the Stampe with makeshift tie-downs, got in touch with the farmer who owned the field, booked us a room at the local, told us to leave our kit with her and invited us back for breakfast. As we were leaving, she brushed aside our words of thanks: "You brought me such memories", she said.

We were up next morning in good time for breakfast, following a quick inspection of the Stampe looking forlorn in the rain. The weather was marginally worse than on the eve, but by mid-morning it still looked very much the same and was reportedly letting up a bit at Redhill.

"Couldn't you just follow the Ashford line back to Redhill?" Mrs Norrie asked, uncannily reading my thoughts. "It's only five miles south of us.... Here let me show you on that map of yours." She cleared a space on the breakfast table to spread the half-mil out and we obediently gathered round her while she briefed us on our return mission to Redhill: "I'll come and see you off", she announced. "Haven't seen a biplane in ages!"

So we trudged back to the field, two goonish figures in Biggles gear escorting a dainty lady in a white raincoat, blue headscarf and matching wellies. The planes seats were brimming with water – we had thoughtfully removed the cushions the previous night and it took a while to bale it all out. To my immense surprise and relief the engine fired up on the first swing. We took off heading south and immediately turned back to make a low pass in front of

Mrs Norrie. She waved excitedly with her umbrella a tiny figure of a woman in the middle of a rainy Kent field alone with her memories of a distant summer and a downed RAF boy.

We found our way back all right – never mind at what height – no not to the hero's welcome I half expected, nor for that matter the carpeting I more than half dreaded. The latter was only a question of time….

Aviation or Flying?

This short article was sent to the Rag by an anonymous American member. It was written by Richard Bach of Jonathan Livingston Seagull fame.

There is a tremendous difference between 'Aviation' and 'Flying', a difference so vast that they are virtually two separate worlds, with precious little of anything in common.

The Aviator finds that after a modest amount of training in the not too difficult mechanics of the airplane and the not too complicated element of the air he can constantly feed his insatiable appetite for new sights, new sounds, for new things happening that have never happened before. In Aviation an aeroplane is a clever, swift travelling device that lets you have lunch in Moines and supper in Las Vegas. The Aviator, then, the faster and more comfortable his aeroplane, and the simpler it is to fly, the better suited it is to his use. The sky is the same sky everywhere, and it is simply the medium through which the Aviator moves to reach his destination. The sky is nothing more than a street, and no-one pays any attention to the street, as long as it leads to far Xanadu.

The Flyer, however, is a different creature entirely from the Aviator. The man who is concerned with Flying isn't concerned with distant places way over the horizon but with the sky itself; not with shrinking distance after an hour's aeroplane travel, but with the incredible machine that is the aircraft itself. He moves not through distance, but through the ranges of satisfaction that come from hauling himself into the air with complete and utter control; from knowing himself and knowing his aeroplane so well that he can come somewhere close to touching, in his own special and solitary way, that thing which is called perfection.

Aviation with its airways and electronic navigation stations and humming autopilots is a science. Flying, with its chugging biplanes and swift racers, with its aerobatics and its soaring, is an art. The Flyer, whose habitat is most often the cockpit of a tail-wheel aeroplane, is concerned with slips and spins and forced landings from low altitude. He knows how to fly his aeroplane with throttle and stick; he knows what happens when he stalls out of a skid. Every landing is a spot landing for him, and he growls if he does not touch down smoothly three-point, with his tail-wheel puffing a little cloud of dust from his target on the grass.

Flying prevails whenever a man and his aeroplane are put to the test of maximum performance. That lonely little biplane way up high in a distant summer afternoon, practising barrel rolls over and over again, is Flying. Flying, once again, is overcoming not the distance from here to Nantucket, but the distance from here to perfection.

Although he is in a very small minority, the Flyer is allowed to walk both his own world and the world of Aviation. Any Flyer can step into the cabin of any aeroplane and fly anywhere an Aviator can. An Aviator, however, isn't capable of strapping himself into the cockpit of a sailplane or a racer or an aerobatic biplane and flying it well, or even flying it at all. The only way he can do this is to enter the same long training that, ironically, transforms him into a Flyer by the time he has gained the skill to operate such aeroplanes.